I WANT TO GIVE YOU AN INCREDIBLE FREE GIFT

Over £500 Worth of Powerful Tools & Resources to Free Your Business from the Exhausting Traps On Its Way to Customer Happiness.

Just go to
www.noelcardona.com/customer-happyland/

CUSTOMER HAPPYLAND

How smart companies design, pick and keep their customers forever!

CUSTOMER HAPPYLAND

How smart companies design, pick and keep their customers forever!

By Noel Cardona

2018

First Printing: 2018

ISBN 978-0-244-98899-9

Noel Cardona Enterprises
www.noelcardona.com/customer-happyland/

To my beautiful Gio. Thank you for making me laugh every step of our journey together.

TABLE OF CONTENTS

PREFACE

It's funny how when you teach something is when you learn the most. We are all teachers, it's just that some people will make it a profession. I say this because when I was doing my preparation for this book and I started collecting my thoughts, resources, looked at my countless days working with customers enquiries and frustrations, as well as what I have learned from customer psychology; I realised more and more that Customer Happiness is not something that is achieved by mistake. It is actually the result of a set of intended and organised actions. It has to do with clarity as to where the organisation is going, the boundaries of the playing field and clear rules.

This book is an unexpected look at what it actually takes to achieve a precious award: the one where your customer chooses you over other possibilities. I say unexpected because you must be able to see the big picture, to be intentional and to have clarity as to what you, as a business, want. Please note that when I say "customer" it can also mean "client".

INTRODUCTION: THE NUMBER ONE THING THAT BRINGS MONEY TO ELITE BUSINESSES

Over my years of work, learning, unlearning, wins and defeats, I have learned that there is a very important reason why money moves from one place to another, it is not the only one, but it is a critical one, want to guess? Have a try... The reason I am talking about is *clarity.* This particular word is responsible for most of the achievement in the world, but especially for the acceleration of achievement. Why would I say that? Because only when we see a clear path we can start moving faster, no human being would instinctively think about running in a place of total darkness unless there is an imminent danger. In the same way, a business will not accelerate until it has clarity about where is going.

Now, the picture does not have to be 100% clear, but there must be a very good sense of such destination. My goal with this book is to effectively help you get that clarity.

There are there levels of clarity a business must have:

1. Strategic Clarity
2. Operational Clarity
3. Ground Level Clarity

Strategic Clarity has to do with what we will be discussing in this book which is specially focused on the subject of Customer Happiness or as I call it CUSH. This type is fundamental to cascade down those few critical actions (20/80 principle) that must be taken to ensure the business gets where it needs to go. If the leaders of a business do not know where they are going, the team actions will follow.

Operational Clarity is the one which ensures all teams and sub teams are going to the same place, pulling in the same direction. In mediocre companies, I very often find that there is a massive misalignment in both, the short and long term across all departments. This is not free and all stakeholders suffer equally because of this reason.

Ground Level Clarity has a dramatic effect on a day-to-day basis. For example, if all your employees know in advance what needs to be achieved in their week and keep them, and others, aligned, such clarity will ensure, if combined with discipline, that such goals are reached. I call this type Ground Level Clarity because is the one that needs to be present on a *minute-by-minute* basis in a business and for that, the goals set must have clear deliverables by the hour. As this is not a time management book, I won't go into detail on this concept but I want you, as a business leader, to keep that concept at top of your mind.

Elite businesses can see with clarity, both internally and externally. Elite businesses prioritize their actions to align them with the big picture. Such businesses know that when they don't have such clarity they are on the agenda of other people, either their customers' or competitors' agenda. In comparison, this is the same that happens to average people: they don't decide what they want to be or become known for, they are the result of other's people agenda, and they are the effect of other's decisions.

I explain this at length because, as I have said before, as a leader you must work every day to get that clarity and equally as important, to transmit that to your team. Now, having said that, let's build a clear picture of what I call "Customer Happyland" looks like.

WHAT CUSTOMER HAPPYLAND LOOKS LIKE

This book was actually inspired by the description I wrote below. My description is intended to give you a vivid picture of where you are going to, a place which mediocre business can hardly imagine.

"Every company and every business leader dreams of being in that place. A place where customers are so happy that they beg you to sell them your products, not the other way around. A company where you are invited in, not one where you force your way in through the door. Sometimes even through the back door. This place is characterised because every member of the organisation moves in synchrony towards a clear goal by using clear rules, even though the path may not be entirely clear. This Neverland of business is one where you can choose which customers you work with and which you don't. Which customers you keep and which ones you fire. Such a place is one where customers will feel guilty if they are not with you anymore, if they don't patronise your business any longer.

Customer Happyland is not necessarily a problem free one; however your customers are raving fans of what you do and will forgive some of your mistakes because they know you care.

In this Happyland, where I am pretty sure, you also want to be, companies already there breathe an air of advancement, optimism, achievement. People continuously ask how we can do this better, instead "We have been doing it like this for years, and it doesn't need changing". The day to day operations is constantly looking to the future not to the past. The collaboration spirit is aided by the understanding that even though they are already there, they need to keep moving because their customers keep moving. Elite businesses can move faster than other companies yet with a lot less friction.

In such place, leaders replace stress with passion for growth and the energy it brings. This energy is the greatest brewing environment for creativity.

However, they also understand that to protect such a place from environmental destruction, creativity must be applied in a controlled manner; otherwise, like fire does to forests, it will destroy what it touches.

You would think that you can arrive at such a place by sheer hard work, however, *it is a place that is designed and then built.* Such act of bravery requires the most precious of assets, after time itself, and that is **clarity.** Clarity on where your company is, where your company is going and how to get there. It is not easy but is not impossible.

Happyland requires great citizens. Members of a society who have what it takes to walk this ancient forgotten path, explorers, if you wish. Because to be at the top, you need citizens willing to open their minds and bring innovation to forgotten lands. Such members must be chosen carefully, as this is critical: for a company outside the borders of Customer Happyland the sum of their parts equals the whole, for companies already there, the collective mind operates at a much higher level, and therefore with more speed. This almost virgin land has a gate where the entry fee is excellence.

The place I describe is one that, for many, is an impossibility, yet many companies are already there. These companies have travelled a long distance from far away. They didn't start there; they came from where you are.

In Customer Happyland, the collective mind works to protect their customers by building moats around their castles, because they know that even though they are strong, enemy armies don't sleep. Because of this, they know they have to keep preparing themselves, learning and not forgetting what they know. They continuously ask how the castle can be strengthened, where the enemies can attack from, when they should attack and how.

This land is the only place where we all are at war, a silent one, yet customers do not suffer any injuries, on the contrary, they benefit by the outcome.

Organisations in Customer Happyland, work as a philharmonic where each instrument is well played and the director can easily draw a beautiful picture of where the music is going, when to up the pace, and when to slow it down. Action coordination is critical.

To get to that place, companies go through three different stages: The Flood, The Re-birth and The Race. I explain this in my book with the same name where I show you the 21 secrets you need to know to get there.

Finally, companies that make it through the Flood and the Re-birth to be at the most exciting stage, the Race, are the chosen ones, who through sheer focus, discipline and the right techniques, can turn their challenges into opportunities, achieving long lasting sound systems which allows them not only to enjoy the luxuries of Customer Happyland but to set the rules by which this kingdom is ruled: they own their industry because their customers are raving fans!"

Now, let's analyse our description of Customer Happyland so you understand better what I mean (again more clarity).

"A place where customers are so happy that they beg you to sell them your products, not the other way around."

Have you ever seen the waiting lines that are created outside the Apple stores when a new gadget is to be released? Some people will even camp for several days to be the first in line, to be the first one to get the phone, the tablet or whatever is being released at the time. Now this effect is only achieved by a combination of different strategies which we will discuss later on, however I want you to focus on one thing here, and that is that Apple almost sells by invitation, they don't really chase customers. Products are normally sold out in a very short space of time.

"This Neverland of business is one where you can choose which customers you work with and which you don't."

Smart companies are purposely designed so not everyone can become their customers. You see, most of us have been taught by the average school of business that the customer is king; however that only applies to businesses which cannot differentiate themselves enough to be able to create a dependency in the customer for the products or services sold. In a smart business, customers actually are not King, the business can actually dictate the path to follow. Companies which know what they are actually doing, can effectively choose which customers they accept and which they don't. Because of these practices, they are able to fire customers and some even go to the extent to show this has been done, in order to educate the rest about what will happen if the rules are not followed.

"...your customers are raving fans of what you do and will forgive some of your mistakes because they know you care."

Elite businesses put all the necessary systems in place to create a community, the best ones at this will be able to develop an almost cult-like movement which becomes part of the life of their customers. The business becomes more than its products or services. You don't have to be Nike or Apple to achieve this, but you need to be smart.

> *"Elite businesses can move faster than other companies yet with a lot less friction."*

As I have said before, for a business to move faster than others, it needs to have clarity. However, as you will see in this book, there needs to be external and internal clarity, external and internal alignment.

> *"...they also understand that to protect such a place from environmental destruction, creativity must be applied in a controlled manner."*

The business, as a whole, understands that in order to create the basis for a long stay in Customer Happyland, it needs to ensure it does not destroys the assets it creates with the substantial effort that it takes to do so. Destroying is easy, building is difficult, but building in the correct way is even more complicated and only elite businesses know how to do it properly. Such business know that nobody can buy the land they occupy at Customer Happyland, businesses can only rent the occupied space. Such rent is paid with continuous focus on maintaining standards because they understand eviction by repeated failure is just around the corner.

"In Customer Happyland, the collective mind works to protect their customers by building moats around their castles".

Outstanding businesses are aware and apply different strategies to keep their customers. Such strategies are a mixture of strong relationships, unique value, membership, expectations management, and ascension strategies, among others.

Traditionally, businesses approach the achievement of Customer Happiness from different angles with unconnected strategies, which is a mistake. Without a sound strategy where you build a frame work to ensure you can design, attract, screen and choose which customers you want to work with, as well as keeping them for as long as you can, achieving customer happiness becomes an utopia. If you analyse companies such as Disney, or seemingly less well-known smaller businesses, which have mastered these strategies, you will realise that their members are actually grateful for being able to belong, to purchase products or services from such an organisation. Some businesses have actually mastered this so well, they charge a fee to customers to just have access to their services, to belong, to see what is inside.

If by now, you are arguing with yourself stating "My business is different I can't possibly do that", I give you two options, one is to stop reading this book and go away or, to open your mind to the concepts I am bringing you here, and identify where your limiting beliefs and inaccurate thinking are stopping you from advancing your business. The growth of any organisation starts with the growth of its members and you are not the exception.

THE FOUR ULTIMATE PILLARS OF CUSTOMER HAPPINESS

We have now seen a summary of the path to achieve customer happiness and if I asked you which you think are the pillars to get there, what would you say? Some people would be tempted to say, the pillars are the layers of the human hierarchy of needs, however, even though I would say that is a close answer it is not the correct one. (We will be discussing the hierarchy of needs shortly).

The pillars of customer happiness, at least from my point of view, are four independent journeys, yet working very closely together, which you must understand in order to get to and stay in Customer Happyland. I define these four pillars as:

a.   Pillar One: The Business's Journey

    b. Pillar Two: The Shareholder's Journey
    c. Pillar Three: The Employee's Journey
    d. Pillar Four: The Customer's Journey

The reason why the pillars come in form of journeys is because of the changing nature of business and people. The pillars talk about a continuous, never-ending process. One that means you can conquer Customer Happyland but you can also be easily expelled if your organisation doesn't pay the price to stay there: **Consistent Business Excellence.**

The four pillars are independent and can remain independent, however in order for your business to achieve CUSH the three journeys need to be understood and combined as much as possible.

Ultimately,

The Business's Journey, leads to operational excellence.

The Employee's Journey, leads to high team performance.

The Customer's Journey, leads to raving fans helping to multiply your business by bringing more customers to you.

The Shareholder's Journey, leads to business stability or the lack of, depending on the vision of the owners.

Let's study more in detail each journey.

THE CUSTOMER'S JOURNEY

(What makes customers happy?)

I hope by now you have a better picture of what Customer Happyland looks like and you are in a better position to move yourself towards that place. (By the way if you wish to get an incredible gift for free please go to www.noelcardona.com/customer-happyland. This gift will give help you to exponentially accelerate your journey towards your business excellence objective). We cannot discuss what makes customers happy without getting into people's minds and the way they think. We all are, after all, suppliers and customers at the same time.

According to Maslow's Hierarchy of Needs presented in Figure 1, all human beings have a group of desires which can be ranked and that are met in an orderly manner:

Figure 1. Maslow's Hierarchy of Needs

After survival (Physiological) needs are met, people will then focus more on non-materialistic things such as Safety, Social/belonging, Esteem and Self-actualisation, the latter having to do with achievement and creativity.

This hierarchy is initially important for you to determine where your products or services are located in the rank and align what you do with your customer's needs. For example, if you are selling fire alarms then you know your customer will look at them from the "Safety" level of the Maslow's Hierarchy; but if you sell concert events, they would be looking at it from the "Social/belonging" tier. Thus hierarchy is probably not a surprise for you, we are all unconsciously aware of this information. However, the trick here is to put it to good use to make a difference to your business.

Over my years of experience, I have divided Maslow's rankings into three specific hierarchies for:

a. Customers
b. Employees
c. Business's shareholders

Let's focus for now on the customer one:

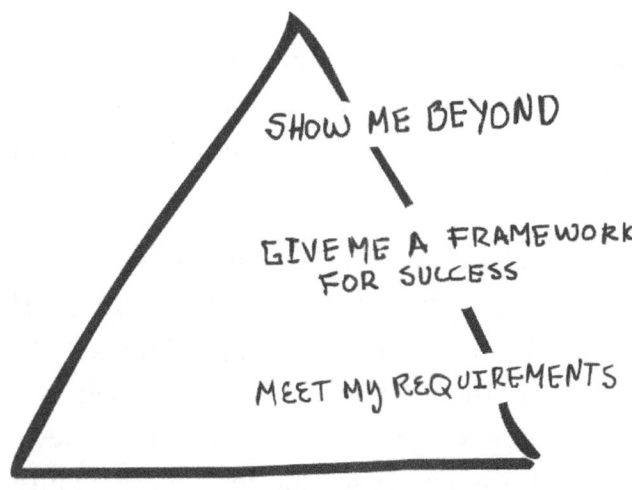

Figure 2. Customer's Hierarchy of Needs

At the very bottom of the hierarchy we have **"Meet my Requirements"**, this means that we all, as customers, want to get what we pay for and no less. Such requirements come in different shapes and forms, and having clarity on what they are is one of the most important pieces of the puzzle for any business to achieve excellence fast! When a business consistently fulfils this tier of the hierarchy, *it basically has a satisfied customer but not yet a happy one.*

The second tier is **"Give me a Framework for Success"**. This tier as such, depending on the business, can be a simple or a complex one to fulfil. What I mean by this is, is that for any product or service provided, your customer wants to have the means for fast and successful implementation. Let's have a look at two examples, a simple and a more complicated one:

Simple Example. If you live in Europe, you probably will know IKEA, which is known for selling cheap furniture. IKEA has been able to gain market share mainly due to the fact that what they sell is not assembled, meaning they save lots of money on storage and transport costs due to reduced volumes: (They can put a lot more products per unit of space in their warehouses or trucks). What this means for their customers is that they have to put their furniture together, which can become very cumbersome. Our Framework for Success question here, is answered by how IKEA's customers are assisted in assembling their furniture. Currently IKEA provides a step-by-step booklet for each item they sell, and from my point of view, I would give them an 8.5 out of 10 score. However, if IKEA wanted to improve on this Framework, they could provide a video. If economics were not a problem, IKEA could have a team assembling for free; however the prices they charge wouldn't allow the business to go to such extent.

Complex Example. An organisation providing coaching services to corporations could just deliver a training program which ensures certain goals of competency are met, i.e., trainees are evaluated and certified to know the key concepts delivered. The Framework for Success here, could be additional support together with the environment required to ensure the trainees can actually introduce these new habits, lessons or practices into their day to day jobs. To do this, the coaching organisation can offer additional programs (which could create additional revenue), a support and collaboration group of other employees from other companies which have already been through the process (a community), additional tools for implementation, etc. In this case, the Framework for Success tier can lead to recurrent revenue for the business, as well as customer happiness because they have the support required to achieve their goals.

This second tier is different for each business, however, is based on the fact that a product or service is always a tool for customers to move from idea to reality, and the more difficult the transition, the more refined the Framework for Success you need to provide them with.

To give you even more clarity on this, the John Maxwell Team is an organisation that provides training for people to become coaches to other people or corporations; because this is such a complex endeavour, once the certification has been completed, people can choose to continue on a program where weekly evaluation and goals are set for them to be able to implement what they have learned, review actions, failures, wins, etc. and then continue with more learning and more implementation. These type of companies have mastered the concept of customer retention (which we will discuss later on in another chapter of the book) because they understand very well this customers' second tier of needs.

The third component to the Customer's Hierarchy of Needs is **"Show Me Beyond".** If you get the whole design of your business right, you will keep your customers for a long time, but if you don't take into account the third tier, you will leave a lot of money on the table and will lose the opportunity to "WOW" your customers and create a cult-like organisation. In plain English, they will get bored and leave.

An example of Show Me Beyond, is the constant innovation Nike takes on to create better trainers, which helps their customers to achieve beyond what they currently can do. This not only stops at selling better trainers, in the Oxford Circus London store I have visited several times (I currently live in London), there is a service to analyse the customer's running technique (those who are willing to pay for it), so they can learn and correct their mistakes and therefore achieve more, run faster, go beyond where they have been before. Psychologically, they will relate their success to your business!

It doesn't matter what business you are in, if you want to retain customers you must focus on improving your relationship with them. One way to do so, is to create unique values which, in many industries, come from this level of the hierarchy.

My Customers' needs Hierarchy summarises many business lessons smart organisations are currently putting into practice. The Meet my Requirements tier is all about Operational Excellence. Customers want everything delivered with no errors and on time. The Framework for Success tier, is all about creating an environment and tools for success: memberships where they get support from you and their peers, boot camps, tools for collaboration, etc. Finally, the Show me Beyond level, is achieved by getting feedback from the collective to satisfy the individual. In other words, to get to know as much as possible your customers' pains and use the business's technical, commercial or social expertise to show them what is next. This is the way businesses can create, and profit, tremendously from new trends.

Even though my Hierarchy of Customer's Needs summarises very well the path to customer happiness, there is something else that needs to be taken into account here, which is the fact that, for any business looking to create customer happiness and the long term retention that comes with it, it must understand that customers only stay long term because of how they feel about themselves when in that relationship with you. In other words, if your Framework for Success does not make them feel great about themselves, about their achievements, if they cannot show off their wins to others in the community created as part of that environment for success, they will leave.

Understanding how average buyers become your best customers is critical for your success: The ones which are most likely to stay for the long term, will get to know what you sell, use it, learn it and if you are lucky, they will become what is known as evangelical customers, raving fans. It is at this point, where it can be seen a lot more clearly, that the status and recognition they get within the Framework for Success, is critical for retention and therefore Customer Happiness.

Conquering Customer Happyland is not possible without having clarity and implementing this Hierarchy. *It is also no possible without understanding the fact that a satisfied customer is not the same as a happy one, and a happy one is different from a raving customer.* Operational Excellence is a must but won't create either happy or raving customers.

THE BUSINESS'S JOURNEY

It is easy to get lost in the day to day operations of your business, especially if you are at the stage of fast growth where not only revenue is rapidly expanding but so is complexity. When you have an organisation with two people, communication can happen in two directions, however, when you go to three people, communication can now go wrong in six different ways, with four people, 12 different ways.

What does have The Business's Journey to do with communication? Well, everything:

Communication is the lifeblood of operational excellence.

Correct? Do you agree? Well not quite, let me rephrase that:

Accurate communication is the lifeblood of operational excellence.

The difference is obvious and significant. I would say that communication is the interchange of information, whereas accurate communication is the successful interchange of information.

Why would this matter you could ask, well, it's because one major part of operational excellence is the absence of errors, and the origin of all mistakes is, in one way or another a break of communication.

One of the businesses which went through my coaching program had as one of their main errors "Wrong product" sent to their customers. Think about that, not late, not scratched, thoroughly the wrong product. Upon investigation this was due to the Sales Department typing the wrong item in their system. This basically meant that what the customer affected wanted (requirements), was established wrongly at the very beginning of the process, therefore there was no way that communication was accurate in these cases, no matter how good this company's systems were from this point onwards.

This basically takes us to the conclusion that all your efforts during The Business Journey, made to achieve operational excellence, must be directed to error proofing such communications.

Another reason why I describe the pillars as journeys is because they have milestones which give us even more clarity as to where to go next. In my book, **The**

Flood, The Rebirth and The Race, I describe the three stages or milestones any business will go through on its way to operation excellence. (I encourage to you read it as well, as it touches on clear techniques necessary for you and your business to grow. Go to www.noelcardona.com/customer-happyland to get it as part of the free gift I have for you).

Let's discuss further these three journey milestones, so you understand where you are and where you want to go next.

THE FLOOD STAGE

This is a stage where most mediocre businesses live. I have called it "The Flood Stage" because these businesses are literally flooded with problems of all sizes: small, large, critical and non-critical. The worst part is that these businesses have no clear visibility of what the main issues are and therefore, everything becomes urgent and requires an immediate response. At this stage employee morale is very low and customer happiness is a utopia because these organisations barely get to have satisfied ones.

Businesses operating at this stage have what I call FUSFA: Fundamental Systems Failures. For example, systems such as very inaccurate stock control where inventory is lost (maybe stolen?). Organisations with FUSFA, describe its knowhow as an art, meaning nobody understands the technicalities of what they are doing so the business is very much at the mercy of experienced employees because if they leave, your product or service won't be produced/delivered.

The vocabulary you hear while at this business becomes common once you have been to several ones: "rework", "recall", "them vs. us" (lower ranks vs. management), "have you got a minute", "Don't change it, it has worked this way for years", "I don't trust the database", "We have received another return", "Thank god it's Friday", etc. I can carry on, but you get the idea.

Flood Stage businesses are characterised because they constantly live in the past, and they have to: the amount of errors that need fixing won't allow for those businesses to even dream about innovation, or growth, let alone being part of the group formed by elite companies which own their industry.

THE REBIRTH STAGE

I call it "The Rebirth" because it's a place where businesses' speed start picking up: businesses still have some FUSFA, but the situation is not as bad as in The Flood. Companies at this stage have set up the systems to manage by numbers not by guessing, and by doing so, they can start making time to remove issues from deep into their system and rely less and less on people decision making.

Companies living in this stage would have happy customers but due to the situation, the vast majority are only satisfied ones.

Businesses here live more in the present than in the past; however, they also battle to stop fires which still happen.

The employees in these organisations have more of a "can do" approach, however, not all the team members are this way, as there will be some who are still mentally in "The Flood". For a business to move from "The Flood" to "The Rebirth" some of the bad performers of your team will have to leave, either by their own decision or, if the business is lucky enough to operate in a legal environment where it can get rid of them easily (think U.S.A) then the change can be achieved faster.

One particular decision for businesses in "The Rebirth" stage, which has a great impact in both the short and long term, is to strengthen their recruitment systems to choose only the best people: one great team member can replace three good ones and 6 bad ones.

Businesses at this stage are slowly changing their mindset from mediocrity to "we can do better", however the mental scars from "The Flood" still persist. Leaders of the organisation start working on internal and external clarity and to error-proof communications across all departments. Such clarity starts with customer needs and staff accountability.

THE RACE STAGE

This is the stage where you want to take your business to.

These companies are not problem free, but the criticality of their issues is low compared to businesses in "The Flood", mostly caused by errors at the very beginning of each major process. For example, input errors where critical information that needs to be transferred from outside of the business to the team making things happen (think about the "Wrong product" example explained above).

A business in "The Race" is a totally data driven one, where decisions are made with facts on hand and if there are none, the team will go and measure to prove there is actually a problem.

These types of organisations spend a big percentage of their time separating themselves from the competition by constantly innovating. Such innovation is fuelled by internal entrepreneurs who are born from an environment which purposely creates leaders and educates them about how new ideas need to be brought into the business without destroying what already exists.

In "The Race Stage" there is no room for FUSFA; this is partly achieved by heavy automation and centralisation of systems both in Sales & Marketing and in Operations. Clate Mask (The co-creator of Infusionsoft), in his book "Conquer the Chaos", describes this best when he discusses how business owners and entrepreneurs (also all the people in your team) will set out to use a different tool for each problem. The issue is that each tool is independent and does not talk to another, therefore creating waste and points of failure. As Clate describes it, "little chaos contributing to companywide chaos".

People working for businesses at this stage know very well the value of their time and practice the Ground Level Clarity concept I discussed in the introduction. This, on its own, is one of the most important precursors for the acceleration of your Business Journey and your arrival to Customer Happyland.

Operational excellence is achieved at this stage and it is fundamental to support all other journeys so the business can truly create Happy Customers. You know when you are doing things really well because you are able to create an almost cult-like group of customers who will help spread the message about how good you are, which in turn will bring you more business and therefore growth.

THE SHAREHOLDER'S JOURNEY

Mike: Hi John, sorry we called without that much of a notice...

John: No problem Mike, how can I be of help?

Mike: John, you know the business is not doing very well in sales and we have to let go the Lab Analyst, unfortunately I need to ask you to take over the workload because we don't have the resources to bring in someone else.

John: Mike, you realise that I have already taken over the Health & Safety role and this would mean that I would be doing Quality, H&S and Lab analysis?

Mike: Yes John, I know that, but still I need to ask you to do it, I don't see any other way.

John: Mike, you know I am willing to help, but in this case, I am not sure if I can do it, and if I manage to do all this work, I certainly won't be able to do it to the standard required.

Mike: In the current situation, we will have to manage to do it this way.

John: Ok, I will give it a go but I would like to review this within the next two months. OK?

Mike: Thanks John for your help. We can certainly review in two months.

The story above was a real one that happened to a team member in a business I was doing consulting for. This person went from doing one job to doing three. Now, the problem is not that an employee can't take a larger workload on, that is what we have discussed when getting great instead of good people; the issue here is that the owner of that business was doing it to improve the balance sheet at any cost so he could sell the business within the next 12 months.

In this case, the business the owner wanted to extract cash as fast as possible from the business with no intentions of thinking about customers, employees or his business journey: a very short term vision aimed to "sweating the assets" of the business.

Once I saw this situation, I decided to fire this customer: if you don't want to do what it takes to transform your business, don't call me, I don't want to work with you.

The story above teaches us an important lesson: there must be alignment among all four journeys in order for the business to create raving fans. The Mike of our story has a short, "at any cost" philosophy, which was in the opposite direction to The Customer, Employees and Business Journey. A company like this is forever doomed to be in "The Flood" stage.

One opposite example to our friend Mike above is one of the businesses I have helped to move to "The Race" stage. When I started working with the management of this organisation, the business was clearly in "The Flood," however the business had been recently bought and merged with another company which made similar products. The new shareholders owned, and still do, a global corporation, with locations in six countries, which is the leader in the world in terms of market share in their industry. The important piece of information here is that the business has been around for 200 years, almost three generations, and they have a long term vision for success. The reason I entered that equation was mainly one: to give them clarity so the alignment of the four journeys could be done as fast as possible. Due to the size of the business, it took three years to achieve this gigantic change, and what an incredible company resulted out of it.

Having those two examples, you can now understand a lot easier my Shareholder's Hierarchy of needs:

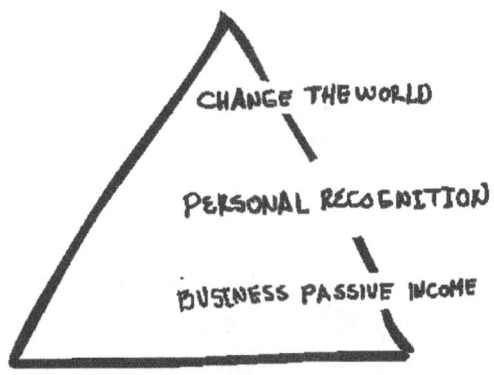

Figure 3. Shareholder's Hierarchy of Needs

The very base of the pyramid starts with **Business Passive Income**, why? Smart business owners aim to build companies which are not only profitable but that also can run themselves. Why? Because they aim to build multiple steams of income and free themselves from the need to work for money and use their time for more meaningful activities. From a shareholder's point of view, the whole business is a vehicle to get from A to B as part of a bigger portfolio or strategy where the owner is looking to profit, in order to create another financial stream so he and his family can achieve financial freedom and all the perks that come with it. A smart business owner will constantly aim to build and delegate systems, so she can fire herself from the equation and go to chase the next dream.

When it comes to tackling the next challenge, the business owner can decide to either keep expanding his empire by growing the business and taking over competitors, or he can decide to sell the business and just cash out his efforts. It is really a personal decision based on his life goals.

Shareholders and business owners are normally high achievers, very competitive people and one way or another love **Personal Recognition.** Their achievements give them just that: the flag they can wave in order show off and be congratulated by other people, hopefully those they admire, because this way, it just feels the dream has come true. Ego is the word here, and we all have it. This is our second tier of the pyramid. Notice that this **Personal Recognition** can come from being able to make the business work, but also there is a different one that comes from working on the next tier of the pyramid.

In terms of our third tier, **Change the World,** the A to B journey we described before, for many, has to do with money, however for a reduced few, it has to do with something bigger, a calling. This is exactly how Tony Hsieh describes it in his book Delivering Happiness, where he talks about his experience at Zappos. A now renowned business for his focus on customer happiness. Tony talks about a point in his business when he had a hard time trying to convince his board of directors (who also were investors), to support additional actions which would greatly enhance the purpose he felt he had to serve: one which would make the world a better place. Tony knew this would become a critical roadblock for the success of Zappos, he decided to buy out the board of directors, freeing the way to live his purpose.

The incredible lesson to take from Zappos' success is that Tony has actually created a movement out of this name "Delivery Happiness", and he and his team go around the United States teaching Zappos' strategies. This seemingly selfless act has actually grown his business reputation, bringing in more customers and powerful investors aligned with his philosophy which is why they accepted the offer from Amazon to take over. The way Tony saw the takeover was not about how much money they would be able to make, but how much bigger of an impact his team could have in the world by having Amazon's systems and support at his disposal.

By now, it should be very clear how the Shareholders' Hierarchy Pyramid and how the type of journey chosen by the owners of the business affects Customer Happiness.

Before we go to our next journey, let me go back to a concept I want to highlight: The short vs. long term vision of a business owner and its effect on the ability of the business to get to Customer Happyland: If we investigate the many years the oldest businesses in the world have been around, the result is jaw dropping. When I heard about this I was thoroughly impressed by the discipline and long term business vision represented for the businesses shown in Table 1. The first thing to notice is that the three shown are over 1000 years old and still operating. That is not 200 or 400 is over 1000! On top of that, they all three are independently owned. The one other important note is that, all three are based in Japan. In May 2008, the Bank of Korea carried out a study including 41 countries which looked for the oldest companies still in operation. Have a look at these numbers:

5,586 companies were older than 200 years.

56% of those companies were based in Japan.

Table 1. The three oldest companies in the world still in operation.

What an incredible feat this is to keep a company running for several generations and privately owned! In order to do this, there needs to be a long term vision, focus and consistency applied to the development of the business, without such discipline in execution and growth, the business, as a whole, will just suffer from "the next shiny object syndrome"

Name	Time Operating (Years)	Industry	Country
Kongō umi Co., Ltd	1,440	Construction	Japan
Nishiyama Onsen Keiunkan	1,313	Hotel	Japan
Koman	1,301	Hotel	Japan

which affects entrepreneurs and business owners during all their careers.

Now the question is, does business longevity equate automatically to Customer Happiness? My answer is not necessarily, businesses are born, they grow and they die. The same as with people, the longer they are on this earth the more likely they are to become complacent, and without constant reinvention, the business will become obsolete. What longevity gives to a business is TIME, which one most important raw materials for achievement. If you contrast the start-ups which are sold 2 years after they were created with the businesses in Table 1, you can easily see how such short tenure will affect the maturity of the systems and vision of the start-up, which will ultimately delay Customer Happyland. The proof of this is that many business take-overs fail because two different cultures clash (normally a bigger corporation trying to introduce a smaller one into its operations) which can easily make the newly acquired start up to go out of business. A long term vision is an important ingredient for great business culture.

THE EMPLOYEE'S JOURNEY

"If you treat them like hell do not expect them to treat your customers otherwise". This is a phrase that still resounds with me from a call with one of my mentors. That single phrase summarises this chapter and you should write it down and keep it close. It is funny how different mentors of mine sometimes express their frustration when it comes to this part of the business:

"If it wasn't for people business would be so easy".

"If I could just replace them all with vending machines".

It doesn't matter how much automation you put in place, you will always need employees. The problem, as usual, is not the people themselves but the programming they come with in their heads. And such programming is due to each individual life journey: where they come from and the environment they grew up as well as the one they currently live in. Even though due to such programming every employee may have different personal goals, in general the hierarchy of needs for them looks like the one below:

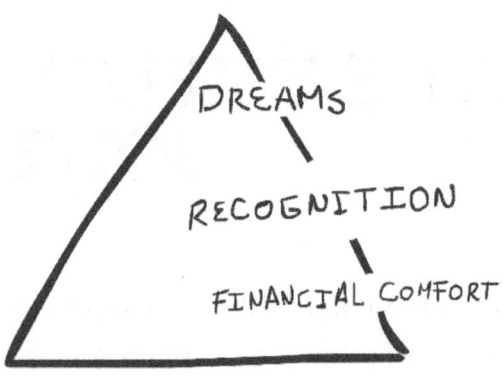

Figure 4. Employee's Hierarchy of Needs

Every employee is on a journey and the business they are working for is a means to an end. You can easily prove that: if you gathered them and asked them to work for free because you cannot make payroll, the vast majority will just leave. It doesn't matter how much they love the business they will have to do so.

An employee by definition is someone who needs financial security or as I call it in the hierarchy of needs, **Financial Comfort**, not just survival. I am not sure who came up with the acronym below, but it is just spot on:

J.O.B: Just Over Broke

Employees are normally fearful of what is out there in the world, if they weren't, they would have their own business and would set their own salary. Such "Financial Comfort" normally turns into an addiction in the form of; "They have to take care of me" which in turn, due to the environment of stability and security, leads people to become comfortable and complacent with no urgency for the business because "my pay check won't change if I do it faster". This entire recipe leads to what I call "Paid Discipline" where rules need to be put in place to make employees productive.

If you don't agree with it, maybe that's because I haven't told you the description above applies to 95% of your employees but not to the other 5%. At least, not in the same way.

Overall, in a business, around 5% of its people are what we could call "stars". Those are the kinds of people that are so good at what they do, that it actually becomes difficult to manage them, because their drive puts pressure to perform even on their own upper management. Each of them, can do the work that would take around 3 or 4 average people. Unfortunately no business can have 100% stars, but they should aim to get as many as possible.

In terms of The Marlow's Hierarchy of Needs for the other 95% of the group, they need **Recognition** continuously just to confirm they are doing well. This is the way to motivate them. The 5% does not need as much paraphernalia because they are self-driven. In the same way, they are not as concerned with the need for Financial Comfort because they know from experience, the value they deliver will get them the salary increases without even asking. A key lesson in the differentiation of both groups is this one:

Self-drive brings more productivity than external motivation.

The top section of the pyramid is all about **Dreams:** a mixture between *personal growth (professional, progression, emotional, etc.) and celebration (holidays, time with family, etc.). Dreams* are different for each employee.

Personal growth is not something you can impose on an employee. The reason why the 5% are so productive in the first place, is because they actively engage in personal development; the 95% will just conform to what the company tells them to do.

If you think about it, in order for a business to conquer Customer Happyland, there needs to be a degree of alignment among all four journeys, and it can be summarised in one word: **Growth.**

During a coaching session with one of my clients, once they expressed their frustration about how difficult is to get people to accept change, to which I quickly replied that is not change what you want, is growth. If they grow, the business will undoubtedly evolve.

What I have described here, is just one Employee's Journey, however there are two different groups which intrinsically have different levels of motivation *to travel the total length of the path.*

A business, in order to ensure acceleration to excellence must develop the systems to bring in such champions. Parts of such systems are recruitment and screening strategies which will allow you to know very well in advance who you are bringing to the team. One such technique is Topgrading from Brad Smart, where a job interview can last for more than a day (sometimes several ones), and the goal being to get to know the candidate very well and definitely discover whether or not he is a good fit for the team.

My point with all of these is that, your employees are on a journey, some of them will have, by default, more stamina than others to get to the top of the pyramid and you always have a choice of which type you bring in.

The employee's and customers' journey have something in common and that is the fact that the trip is more mental than physical. (This will be more evident later on in the book). This is the reason why we have recognition in the pyramid as a tier. The connection between your 5% champions and the mental journey is that, as Kelly Matthew, author of the book "The Dream Manager" says, "An employee is only engaged if she believes her future is bigger than her past". And your champions clearly understand this and know that their biggest impact in their future can be done by their own work. As obvious as it is, your 95% won't see that.

Now, always remember this: employees see companies as vehicles to get them closer to their dreams. The more an employee relates to the business they are working for, to the means to achieve what they want in life, the more the difficulty of the job at hand will move to a second place, and the more productivity your business is going to get. This is the reason why you must install systems in your business to find out what those Dreams are and give extra help (mentorship is one possibility) for your people to move faster towards those as well. Do you have any such systems?

Why does all this matter in our quest for Customer Happyland? Because how your employees feel and act affects your customers directly or indirectly:

- The higher the Morale, the bigger the pride of working in your business.
- The stronger the belief that your business will make their future bigger, the longer they will stay.
- The bigger the sense of financial comfort, the harder they will work.
- The bigger the sense of recognition, the higher the sense of "I am happy in this place".
- The more opportunity they have for growth, the more likely they are to engage in personal growth.

This in turn will translate to how they interact with your customers and how they are engaged to push your Business Journey towards Business Excellence.

CREATING CUSTOMER HAPPINESS IN ADVANCE

"...Southwest Airlines delivers the least, it is a god-awful experience from beginning to end, you know that if you are not there 2 hours before, you are going to have the orange pass and will end up in the middle seat between two people eating buckets of chicken and that's how you are going to fly across the country... for years you've got no amenities, no nothing, you get a crappy little seat... however, year after year, they have the highest customer satisfaction and they deliver the least, if American Airlines treated them as Southwest Airlines does, they would be burning down the terminal, Southwest does it, they are happy. Why? Because Southwest manages their expectations to start with..."

Dan Kennedy
Business and Marketing Guru

I have always said that, we all, as customers, are merciless: we get angry when we don't get what we paid for, and some people can get emotional to the point of being rude. If we analyse the actual reason why we get angry, I would argue that there two sides to this coin: one of them is the fact that customers are promised certain things which they come to expect. Within those promises there are core needs and supplementary ones. In the example of Southwest Airlines the process looks like this:

- You are going to come but no seat will be assigned.
- You are going to stand in line and will give you a plastic pass.
- We will call you by groups and you will all stampede to the plane as a herd, elbow each other out of the way and get the best seat you can fight for.
- We will fly you across the country and will give you a bag of peanuts and a coke.
- We will take off on time and we will get you there on time.

You would wonder how on earth Southwest can manage to sell the services having the picture above and why people would stand it? Probably you already know the answer from our example in the beginning:

Southwest can do it because they have been very clear with customers about what they are and what they aren't. They have a promise to take you from A to B on time, they achieve operational excellence so they keep that promise and they manage expectations about what is not core.

By the way, if you look deeper into the paragraph above, you will see how all four journeys start connecting to each other:

- Operational Excellence is needed to keep promises. Such operational excellence involves the business' and Employee's Journeys.
- Core promises made to customers must be in line with the state of their own current journey (their needs).
- The whole thing must perform to a level serving the needs of shareholders (financially and perhaps, create recognition and have a positive impact in the world, not all business owners want to go the whole way up the pyramid).

Now, going back to the Southwest example and quoting Dan Kennedy again:

"The lesson of Southwest is people will tolerate anything if their expectations are properly managed about what it is they are going to tolerate".

Having said all of this, customer happiness can, and actually must be, created in advance by introducing activities in your business that lead to several critical outcomes:

- Your Marketing and Sales department (M&S) must clearly understand the promises the business is making to ensure that they are in line with customer expectations.

- Your M&S must also make clear what customers won't get and any other non-core expectations that must be managed.

- Your other departments must also understand such promises and ensure that, if something is out of reach then it is fed back to M&S or investments are made (Shareholders' Journey Aligned with all others) in order to bring in such capability.

- There is accurate "management and communication of promises" so all teams are aligned for every order placed. In other words, if you cannot deliver in two days then don't promise it, but if you can, make sure everyone knows it needs to be delivered in that time frame.

Getting to Customer Happyland is therefore an exercise that is done way before you get an order. One that is about focusing on the promises you make to customers: knowing what your core business is and what it is not, delivering every time on your core promise and removing the secondary promises which can drain your resources (think money and time) and damage your reputation.

CREATING CUSTOMER HAPPINESS THROUGH DEPENDENCE

We have already discussed the fact that The Customer Journey is more of a psychological one, and that is the reason why you can create happiness in advance as we discussed before.

There is clear evidence that when given too many choices, people simply do not value what is offered. In more technical terms, the Offer and Demand balance moves to the side of customer power. When people can see that there is plenty of a resource, the amount wasted of that resource automatically increases; a good example is that in London it is said that we waste 30% of the food we eat or order, why does this happen? Because people believe is an infinite resource, cheap and they can get it easily.

I come from Colombia and not from a rich family, even though my country has plenty of food the gap between poor and rich is wider than in Europe and therefore many people struggle more to survive a. Food is definitely not wasted as much over there. It definitely hurts me when we waste food at home and is basically connected with where I come from.

When you first picked up this book, you read on the cover "How smart businesses design, choose and keep customers forever" this chapter relates directly to the "Design" part, why? Because you must purposely design your business to create Customer Happiness through dependence: this is a critical step to the whole processes. By doing this, you will exert control and remove yourself from the mediocre group of businesses which state that "customers are king", let me repeat that:

You must design your businesses so you can exert control over your customers and escape from the mediocre bunch that believes "Customer is King".

The paragraph above will pay for this and many books to come, houses, boats and all your luxuries. I am not joking!

The main strategy to create dependence is differentiation in what your value is. As I said before, when people are given too many choices, they just will not value what you offer, after all, they can go and get it anywhere else and you have no way to control that customer. As usual, there will be many people who believe this is just the market's fault because it is incredibly competitive, however, let me break the news to you, it is your fault. There are many ways of differentiating your business ranging from the simple ones to the very complex ones.

Simple Example: I started out in Chemical Engineering where, very early, I learned one of the main strategies to create differentiation: to give commercial names to simple and mundane chemicals so customers cannot easily switch to a different supplier, of course, you can request information as to what is in the product, however, from the information you will get, the exact recipe of what you are buying won't be clear. This strategy extends into the labelling of common products which describes composition in a vague manner. This simple practice generates a barrier for switching to the competition. A particular company I worked with, had a single product with five different names, each one used in separate industries. The reason? Different industries will pay different prices.

As incredible as it is, the simple use of a different terminology than what your peers use in your industry, can help avoid commoditisation of what you sell, because your customers have no easy way to Google what you do and get a different quote for it. In fact, in marketing, this vocabulary is important to start creating a community and get the people talking and quoting your made up words. One of the main ingredients of a closed community is that they have their own language and that starts right here with this strategy.

If you think this only applies to manufacturers think twice, in his book "Trust Based Marketing", Matt Zagula, explains that in his industry, Life Insurance, common terms are for example: mutual fund, annuity, life insurance, living trust, etc. Due to the need for people to use these terms to start their own research, he has simply renamed all the processes in his business so customers are immediately locked to his business.

Another way to create customer happiness through dependence, a more complicated one, is to come up with new products which can be protected by law-like patents or other means. A patent will normally give you about 18 years protection. If you combine this capability with a good vocabulary and managing customer expectations you will have a great opportunity to have happy customers, ideally paying on a recurrent basis (more on that later).

Designing your business to create customer happiness is not easy but it is a critical pillar for your business to rise above mediocrity. And by the way, mediocrity is a comparative term: If you were alone in your industry, there would be no way of knowing whether you are mediocre or not, in this case you would be the only option.

When you manage to create "perceived unique value", something your customer thinks she won't get anywhere else, that is the point where you can start exerting control and, like a doctor, you start prescribing and not selling: elite businesses in any industry have the luxury of prescribing instead of selling.

PICK WHICH CUSTOMERS YOU WORK WITH

Happiness is a mental journey, and Customer Happiness is no different. By now, you probably understand this very well.

We explored the concept of commoditisation by perception before, now I want you to think about what happens when you really want something but you can't have it? You probably go crazy, and even other concerns like price, go to a second place. You are not alone in this, it is basically a common behaviour of a society who has learned to have anything they want and, worst of all, have it instantly.

The way smart businesses design and pick their customers is, first of all, clarity on who they want to attract and second, they set up processes by which only prospects with such qualities will be able to make it through their gates. In order for this to happen, certain things must be in place already:

a. The perception of unique value we have already discussed.
b. Accurate description of who you want to work with.
c. A community of like-minded people which your prospect will access.
d. A process to ensure your prospect has to ask you to sell what you are offering.

Point a, we have already discussed in another chapters. Let's talk about the other ones.

ACCURATE DESCRIPTION OF WHO YOU WANT TO WORK WITH

This stage of the process also belongs to the "Create Customer Happiness in Advance" concept. The reason I say this is because, if you are making a party and invite moaners and negative people, you are in for a very bad time. If your "Customer Recruiting" process is well designed then you should be attracting the people you want and, as much as you can, the ones that you don't.

Successful businesses, once they have been able to connect with a prospect, will do their best to make sure the new potential client knows the rules through which the organisation operates and, if this new person does not feel comfortable, then is constantly reminded he can (and should) leave. I call this Customer Recruiting because it works almost in the exact same way as Employee Recruiting: You only want the best to come in.

Think about this, a constant in the majority of businesses, is the finite nature of their resources, especially to get new customers. If you allow bad customers to get into your business world, they will only create waste. By the same token, if you are not good for them and therefore reject them, you won't waste their time anyway. It is actually a win-win. As a leader, you must figure out what is not a good customer for you and then don't take them.

A COMMUNITY OF LIKE-MINDED PEOPLE

In my mind, it is more difficult to get a new customer than it is to retain it.

When I described The Customer Journey, I didn't mention the fact that it is also called this because, whatever you are selling to her, is a tool to help her get from A to B, from idea to reality (the same as in our Shareholder's Journey). My whole point with this is the fact that, more than a product or service, your customer craves results, therefore you need to provide the "The Framework for Success" that I discussed in the Hierarchy of Needs for your customer.

One of the most important tools for you to create such a framework is a community of people dealing with the same challenges. This part of the framework works in several ways and has several benefits such as:

- Customers will share information on the implementation of the product which may not be entirely clear from the initial instructions you have provided.
- It can be used to communicate constantly with your community and a lot more easily.
- You can listen to their conversations directly and improve your offer from what you hear. Also to act quickly on any negative trends.
- Your most loyal customers will cross-sell your products, by giving testimonials and feedback many times without your intervention.

- Friendships start to be created, taking your customer relationship program to a different level: a "family" starts being born.

Due to all these characteristics, creating a community as part of your framework for success is a massive tool for customer retention, however, it's not the only one.

Managed properly, you can increase the perceived value of such a community by:

- Only allowing people who meet certain characteristics to belong, in other words you pick who comes in.
- Setting the profile of your average member very high so you can actually start charging for ongoing access to such community.
- With a high access fee, you create recurrent revenue as well as educating people about the intrinsic value of what you are selling: If you are too cheap people won't value what you do.
- Educating your customer on rules about leaving the community. For example, a rule of a coaching community to which I belong, is that if you leave the group (you cancel the subscription), you won't be able to come back.

Do you remember I told you about the fact that The Customer Journey is a mental one? Well, what I just described is a good sample of that: a mental journey you can design and shape to your benefit.

If you are good at spotting patterns, you will have realised by now, how the different journeys mixed with other basic ingredients create a dynamic for customer happiness.

A PROCESS TO ENSURE YOUR PROSPECT HAS TO ASK YOU TO SELL HIM WHAT YOU ARE OFFERING.

We just discussed this a little bit, but let's expand more on it because it is very important.

If you have done things well, your prospects will have a perception of your unique value (even if it's not unique) and this can be used in order to delay the sales process...wait a minute, did I say "delay the sales process"? Is it not the opposite of what we want to achieve? Well, not if you want to be able to create a happy customer which you can control.

Now, there is a lot more to it than just a community, there also needs to be a path in your business for prospects to move from "new to the business" to "paying customer" to "raving fans". This is a critical part of the puzzle we will review later in the book. For now let's assume you have done all your work and you have your prospect ready to ask you to sell to him. What you need to do is to create an application process by which you tell him what will take for you to let him in, and for him to justify why he meets those criteria and any other reasons why he thinks he is fit to belong to your business.

Again, the criteria for customer or client acceptance must be based on what you want to achieve within the Framework for Success that you have envisioned. I have seen examples such as:

a. "You must have an operating business and revenue of 100K per year".
b. "You must be a Certified Accountant with a salary of over £80K per year".
c. "You must be male and pay £25K entry fee to belong to this club".

One of the end goals here, is to create exclusivity (not everyone can enter) and to set a picture of what your future client will get: all this increases the perceived value of your business and offer.

THE HIDDEN SECRETS TO CUSTOMER RETENTION

We have discussed how you can design and pick your customers, we have also said that you need to envision and arrange your business in a way you can gain control over such customers. There is a dichotomy in all this process which seems to contradict itself but it actually doesn't:

You must ensure you satisfy and wow your customers, to help them as much as you can, however you are not responsible for their results even though you provide them with the best Framework for Success that you can. Also, working towards Business excellence and Customer Happiness is not about servitude, it's about, again, efficiency and control.

You would think that getting customers to stay forever is a matter of giving them more a better value, but that may not be the case and you could quite cause the opposite: you can saturate them and they will leave because they may feel overwhelmed and just leave you to release the pressure.

We discussed the concept of Customer Journey already but there is something I have not told about yet: There are two types of Journeys that any customer will be travelling at any given time: The External Customer Journey and The Internal Customer Journey. We have already talked about the former with our hierarchy of needs; let's take some time to talk about the latter.

THE INTERNAL CUSTOMER JOURNEY (ICJ)

This journey is critical because it's the one that you can affect directly and the one you have 100% control to specially implement retention over.

The ICJ is the one that comes in contact with the other three journeys and where the alignment of all four is tested. In other words, as your customer travels through your system, they will quickly notice how happy your employees are, what the shareholders vision is and which stage your business is on its way to Customer Happyland (or to the lands of the Flood).

The ICJ starts with your sales funnel and, if designed properly, will fall into an ascension ladder. It looks something like this:

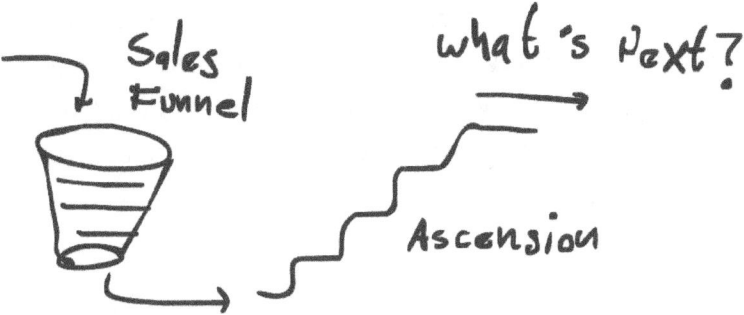

Figure 5. Internal Customer Journey

Just as a reminder, this book is doing something that other books wouldn't normally do: connecting Operational Excellence with Sales and Marketing. Why? Because to achieve Customer Happiness, as I have said before, both must work together in synchrony. Normally with S&M dictating what needs to be done and Operations doing what is necessary, however, no promises should be made to your customers which you know you won't be able to fulfil. Note that for companies in the Flood, operations normally dictates what Sales and Marketing should do, limiting the business to what its leaders want instead of customers' desires.

SALES FUNNEL

Now back to our Internal Customer Journey. If you are not familiarised with what a sales funnel is that is ok. A brief explanation is this: *It is a system designed to incrementally increase the trust your prospect has in what you offer, to the point where you can convert that prospect into a paying customer.* It looks like this:

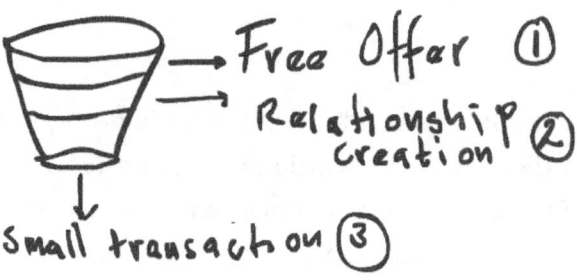

Figure 6. *Sales Funnel Structure*

A sales funnel can become very complicated; however, in my am just showing it in three steps which are, from my experience, it's one of the most important building blocks. Let's have a look.

Free offer: As you are looking to bring a new prospect to your world, a prospect you already have a defined profile for, you have to confront the crude reality:

that person does not know you and does not trust you or what you do. By the way, trust is necessary for customer satisfaction but is not enough for customer happiness, for that you need admiration of some kind, from them towards your business.

Businesses have therefore designed a free offer which could be a free trial or a free gift which tackles that first hurdle of "I don't really trust you" and to start showing that prospect what you do and provide value at the very front to:

a. Get them to explore what you do and decide you have the solution they are looking for.
b. Start repelling those who do not fit the profile you are looking for.
c. Start educating them about what is next and about your entire Framework for Success.

By the way, even to give them a free offer, you still have a hurdle of trust, which means you have to convince them that it is actually free!

Relationship Building: If done properly, your free offer should have let you get the prospect's contact details so you can start communicating regularly (as often as possible) with them, to continue building trust and further educate them, provide value and building some basis for the control you will exert. For example, a way of communication could be daily emails, within those emails you can discuss examples of actual customers you have fired and why it was done, hopefully connecting that to the rules you have for your business and that eventually you want them to follow. The continuous incremental increase in trust will lead to the next step in the funnel.

First Small Transaction: If your business has done things well, your customer will, when they are ready, trust you enough to invest in your offer. By now they will assume that you will deliver as promised, but you need to make sure you do, otherwise all the work you have done so far will be lost. Once this milestone has been reached, you can start educating and preparing this buyer to get into your ascension path.

When I talk about controlling customers and the fact that your business should not fall into the trap of "servitude", many people feel uncomfortable and it's understandable, the business education they have received in the past is what makes them feel this way. If you want to bring your business to Customer Happyland you must start with unlearning anything that will sabotage the path of your organisation.

ASCENSION PATH

Keep their mind and eyes busy and they will stay with you. Now this statement is not 100% accurate but is pretty close. One of the main strategies to do that is an ascension path.

Average ascension paths would have at least two steps and it can go as complex and extensive as the one shown for Amway in Figure 9 (page 91), a multilevel business. There is no argument that those levels are designed for the people working for Amway,

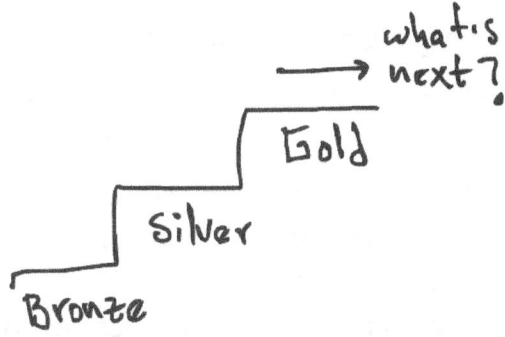

Figure 7. Example of Ascension with three levels

However, if you know these types of businesses, those same people need to become customers first in order to climb the ladder.

In Figure 7, I show a path for which there are three different levels. Normally, in the industries which have already been using this for a long time, the first level is free but then the benefits and the costs on each level increase. One of the main benefits is the fact that "sub communities" within the community you have created are formed following the normal path of stratification in any society: the ones at the top are more successful and therefore the ones at the bottom want to get there. If handled well, the ones at the very top will help pull customers from the bottom (think "internal testimonials") accelerating and increasing revenue for the business. At the same time, it creates a sense of achievement for your customers which is ultimately what get them to stay.

THE LINK BETWEEN BUSINESS SUCCESS AND CUSTOMER RETENTION

If you have been paying attention, you will notice that there are four concepts that have appeared during our discussion, which are effectively the link between the success of your business and the retention of your customers. Figure 8 shows what I call "The four loops concept".

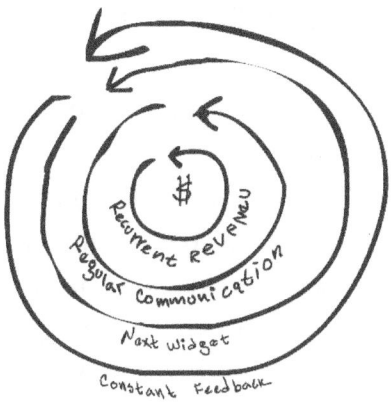

Figure 8. The four loops Concept

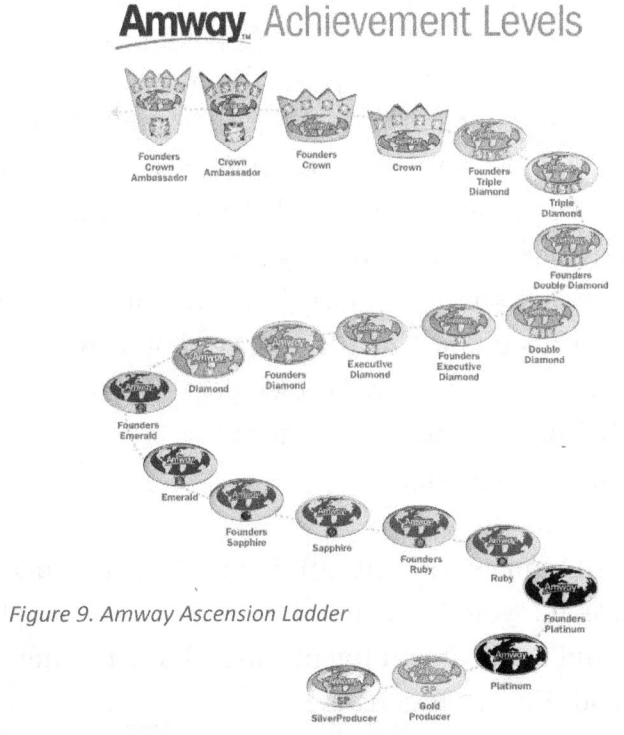

Figure 9. Amway Ascension Ladder

Loop 1: Constant Feedback. All you are doing in your business is a big and constant experiment and you know you have arrived when you can measure the response of your customers, it could be money or it could be another metric, and you confirm that the goals you were looking for is what the numbers are telling you. Installing systems in your business to constantly get this feedback, is one of the most important actions you can take, so your whole organisation can determine whether or not ideas are worth pursuing.

Loop 2: Next Widget. This is a concept embedded into the sales funnel and the ascension path. It is essentially a never ending exercise (a loop) to find the next product that can serve your customers. Working on this cycle can be tremendously challenging, because you must be constantly bringing new ideas to your customers in a form they have to pay for. By the way, when I say new "ideas", I am not necessarily speaking about new to the market but new to your customers. It can even be old ideas your customer already knows about, but dressed in a way that make them more appealing.

When it comes to determine your next widget, I recommend you look at other industries, adapt to yours and innovate on top of those. I don't remember who said this but it is true:

"Innovation starts with imitation."

Loop 3. Regular Communication. This loop holds a very important concept, one that you must not forget about: ***most customers leave businesses because they are neglected***, because, as we have discussed before, business leaders have a mindset of "single transaction", so they don't see the need for regular communication. If you don't have an ascension path or a funnel, you won't see the need for regular communication either. Businesses in "The Flood" stage will just say "We are too busy; we don't have the resources to do that". Ironically, they have the resources to go and find new prospects, which is more expensive and difficult than creating regular communication to your existing list. Do you see why I say "The Flood" stage is basically a hamster wheel where business leaders are continuously chasing their tails?

Regular Communication is critical for several reasons:

- The obvious one is, you need to keep on top of your customer's minds, your face on the window if you wish, for the next time they need you.

- You can provide ongoing value through your communications and as part of your framework for success.

- You can educate them and constantly challenge their thinking so you prepare the land to bring your offers in.

- You manage their expectations to create customer happiness in advance as we have already discussed.

- Continue to repelling "out of profile" customers, therefore increasing the value of your community reinforcing the foundations of "like-minded" people.

Loop 4. Recurrent Revenue. If you have set up the ascension path correctly, you should be able to frame it into a Recurrent Revenue model, which works in tandem with which we have already described:

a. Regular communication.
b. Membership based organisation.
c. Additional revenue from new, one off, widgets.

The last one is very important because by doing so, you start creating multiple sources of income from the same client, which enhances even more your capacity to align all four journeys and therefore increasing the speed towards "The Race" stage.

As a leader of your organisation, you must be continuously running all four loops. This is critical on the road to Customer Happiness.

CUSTOMER'S FEELINGS JOURNEY

Continuing with the process of designing your organisation for Customer Happiness, let's now direct our attention to how you purposely ensure that the

Figure 10. Customer "Feeling Journey"

internal customer journey (ICJ), is the one that you want. In other words, this is how you ensure excellence is not left to chance.

There in an ideal "Feelings Journey" your customer should have, and which is shown in Figure 10, as it interacts with your business. Let's have a look in detail:

Fear. When your customer doesn't know you or knows your product or service, there is fear. Fear of making a bad decision, or investing in the wrong solution, whether or not it is going to work. It is definitely the lowest point in your relationship with them.

Uncertainty. At this point your customer has taken the free offer or heard from you in a different way, so now more than fear, there is uncertainty, because there is doubt whether or not you have the capacity to deliver, whether or not you will help in case things go wrong.

Low Level Trust. Potentially at this point your customer has invested in one of the "low price level products" (Do you have one?) designed to move them to this milestone. This is a big jump and is the point where you can demonstrate that you can deliver.

Satisfaction. This comes when you deliver on that first offer and the subsequent ones. Satisfaction is the result of increasing the trust level by fulfilling what was promised.

Happiness. Happiness comes after satisfaction because is generated by providing "perceived high added value", in other words, your customer does not expect it, and even if for the company it does not represent a significant value, for your customers, it may mean a lot. An example is Zappos, which we have discussed before; they upgrade customers to overnight delivery on top of their offer of free delivery for their orders. Happiness, as we have endlessly discussed by now, is a mental journey, and making a big thing out of a small upgrade, helps Zappos amplify the WOW effect they want to create.

Another important part of the Customer Feelings Journey is the peace of mind at the back of their heads, from knowing you will help when things go wrong. A good example of this is Amazon. Just now I have complained to them because one item purchased from the USA (I live in London) was delivered but left outside the building. Unfortunately it looks like somebody took it. When I wrote to them, the first thing they told me was "Don't worry, we take full responsibility for all items". So in advance, I know that my problem will be sorted. When you provide the right help in times of worry for your customer, the impact on them can be twice or three times bigger than the one you caused just by meeting their requirements.

Arguably, this peace of mind part of the puzzle, starts at the "Satisfaction" level but as I said, it plays a critical role at "WOWING" your customer.

Devotion. Devotion comes from uniqueness. Unique value, or the perception of it, combined with all other characteristics is required to achieve customer satisfaction and customer happiness. This stage is an extreme example of the amplification of how your customer sees you; all this is built on strong foundations which guarantee business excellence. Otherwise you would just be faking it.

To create a customer devoted, cult-like organisation it is necessary to:

a. **Focus:** on a section of the market where you can create a likeminded community which will fuel the amplification we are talking about. Bear in mind that the bigger the community the more difficult is to handle it, however it still can be done. One of the communities I belong to is now international, and handles this via individual chapters in different cities. You know is going well when people start calling the community a "family".

b. **Make it personal:** In order to get to the devotion level, is necessary for people to personally connect with the business, and not just see a faceless organisation they trade money to for products. The whole point with the "Feelings Journey" I described before, is for you to connect the dots and see that happiness is an emotion and the contact with your customers' needs to move towards that level. The best people I know doing this are entrepreneurs, (I am one of them). Because they are often a one man van, they must directly handle communications with their customers, and in order to make it effective, to grow a community, they share personal stories, struggles, life experiences, etc. combined with business value. On the other hand, big businesses tend to lose the capacity to do so and therefore they hire celebrities or recognised personalities to become the face of their company. I am still to be convinced that is the best way to put a face to your business.

c. **Consistency.** My fee per day of consulting is £6,000, however I will give you a big piece of advice for free: **Success is rented.** This is directly related to your Business Journey, where all operational excellence is directed to achieve consistency, in other words, right first time every time. Businesses, the same as people, get distracted and can lose their consistency very easily; that's why businesses can travel from "The Flood" to "The Race" stages and still can go back if they are not careful. I have always said that customers do not fully forget mistakes: they will accumulate them at the back of their mind and keep score. I have said before that happy and devoted customers are more likely to forgive issues, however, give them enough problems and they will start thinking your business has lost its edge. Always remember: Customers are merciless!

d. **Bring the community together.** In short, grow the sense of "family". Let me explain this with an example. www.reedsdiary.com is a small business, which is slowly growing in the market of delivering milk door to door directly to consumers. One on the activities they do every year is to bring all customers together for a "Customer Appreciation Event", designed to thank the people who support the business for their loyalty. The company assumes all expenses and their customers have a fab time. The employees get to interact with their customers directly, as well as there is a lot of interaction between different customers. If done well, an event like this is not only useful to say thank you, but to potentially bring new referrals and market new products. My point here is that during an event like this the sense of community is enormously enhanced.

If you want your business to create devoted customers you must find ways to show your appreciation and to bring them together, and even for paid events, the effect is similar.

e. **Tell your story:** Many experts would argue that feeling part of something bigger is the most critical part of CUSH, but I would be tempted to say that all the ingredients we have discussed are equally important.

When I say tell your story (or the business's one), I am talking about your past story and your future one. The past one we discussed about on our "Make it personal" section. The future one is what your business stands for and where it is going, this will help you connect to your community even more and make it easier for you to bring in new members.

In a later chapter I will be discussing more techniques to ensure you are rapidly moving customers from Satisfaction to Devotion.

MAP OUT YOUR CUSTOMER'S INTERNAL JOURNEY

One of the things I would like you to see is the fact that I use the word "journey" a lot in this book to highlight the fact that a business is dynamic, never static, which is what businesses in The Flood either blindly believe or thoroughly ignore.

Successful businesses (and people) focus their actions at the "cause" side of the equation not at the result. This chapter is exactly about that: *you must define and work towards building the exact path you want your customers to follow during their ICJ as they interact with your organisation.* The best tool you can use to do so is Customer Experience Maps (CEM).

CEMs are not a simple thing to do, however you should start from the big picture and drill down as deep as you can. With every layer you dig, you will find additional insights, which will accelerate the achievement of your business's goals.

As a general framework, a process map has at least five components which are critical for your business to see with a lot more clarity (again that word) the trip your customer is on, what they are feeling and how you can help them. If done correctly, this exercise should uncover opportunities which can give you an edge over your competition.

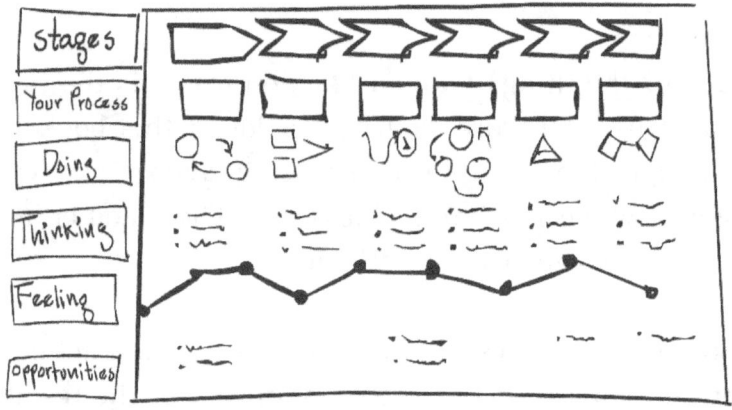

Figure 11. Customer Experience Map

Stages (Their process). These are the stages of the journey that your customer is taking to get the solution they want, in other words a high level description of the process that will take them from A to B. For example, if you have a travel agency, the journey may start at "Desire for Travel" and may end at "Remember the Experience". I use the word "may" because it is for your business to decide how much of that trip you want to cover. Walt Disney used to think in terms of the "Whole Package" which, in practice, would mean that Disney aims to cover as much as practically possible of the stages a customer goes through, from the point they want to have some holidays, to the point they leave the parking lot at Disney.

See Figure 12 for an example on a CEM for rehash.org, a company working towards the use of organic waste as fertiliser.

Your Process. Once you have determined the Stages of your customers process to get from A to B, you can include, below each stage, how your business processes are currently working (or not), in alignment with your customer journey. In this section, you can use your sales funnel framework for the very beginning of the process and then as ICJ starts going deeper and deeper, you can include what are known as "touchpoints", which are steps where your customer is directly in contact with either, your people or your processes. Bear in mind that, even though, not all your departments may appear on this part of the map, it is a fact that everyone in your business affects customer experience either directly or indirectly.

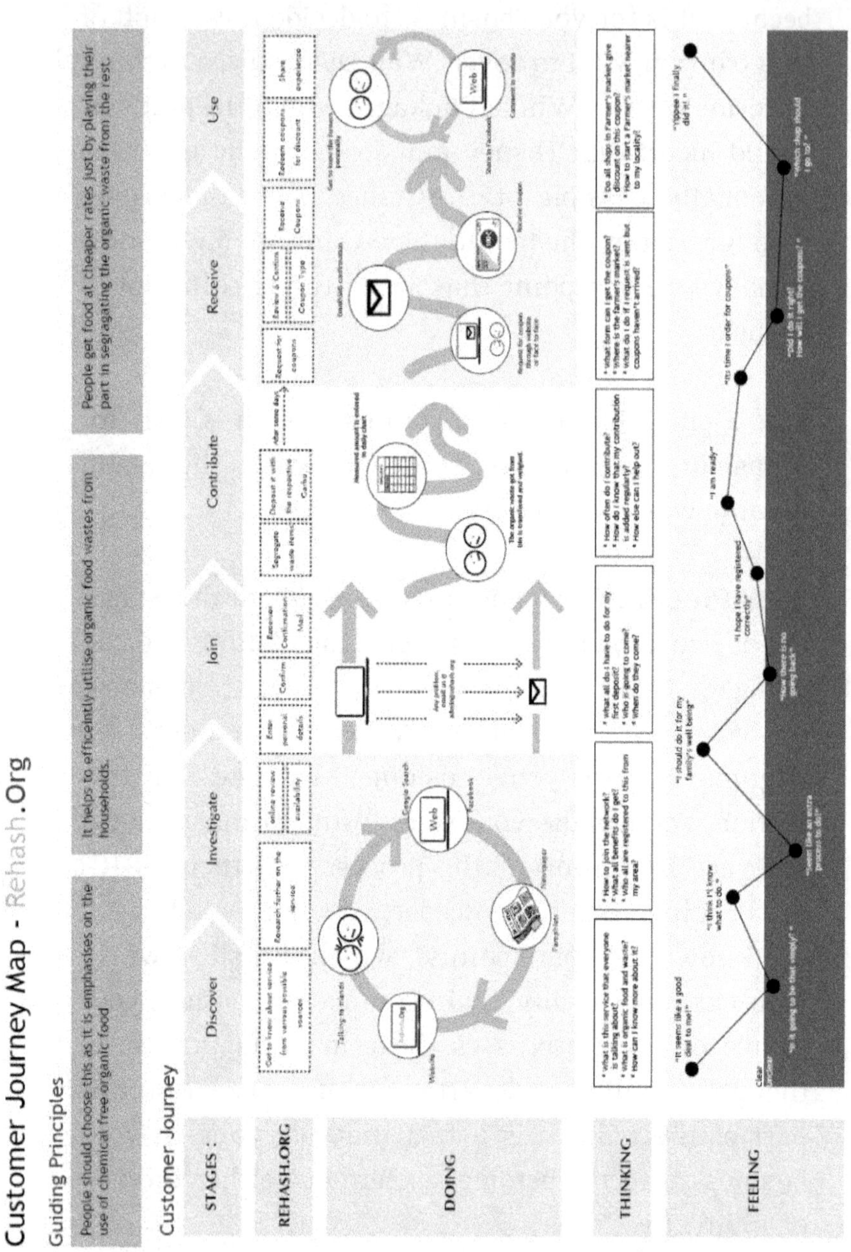

Figure 12. Customer Experience Map from Rehash.org

As you can see by now, this is an exercise that can get very complex and you could use a whole wall, a page per stage, etc. The ultimate goal here is you get into your customer's head to extract critical information necessary to improve your operations.

Doing. This section looks to identify which activities and how your customer goes about each stage in order to get closer to their goal. For example, when your customer initially comes up with the need to travel, they will start researching via web, or call an agency to give them advice as to where they could go, or if they have a more clear idea, they will look for the best agencies for that particular kind of trip. (Somebody they can trust).

Connecting this with another section of the book, you should not limit this map to what is supposed to be happening, but also what you want to happen. *That is why you must do this exercise at least twice: one for your current state and another one for your future one.* The latter should allow you to create the means for you to exert the control over your customers which we have already discussed.

Thinking. This section is also very important because we must be able to formulate the questions your customer is asking himself. Such questions are very closely linked to the Feelings Journey we discussed in an earlier chapter. Questions such as Can I really trust this business? Do I really want to change suppliers? What do I get by doing so? If the product stops working, do they have a guarantee to cover? Make sure you spend enough time here because the insights you will get can become an asset for your Marketing Department. By the way that section of your business would be best named as "Expectations Management Department".

A good way to find out about what your customer is thinking during the different stages, is to go to online forums, read reviews, using surveys and focus groups, etc. It could also be first-hand experience from when you have gone through similar processes before.

Feeling. Put yourself in your customer's shoes and write statements in the form of questions such as "I am not sure if I want to try a new provider", "Why is contacting you so difficult, does this mean their customer service is poor also?" etc.

The Thinking and Feeling stages are almost at the end because by then, you will have a clear picture of the whole journey, which will enable you to identify a lot easier, the emotions currently involved and the ones that you want to create.

Opportunities. This section is basically the gap you need to fill or any ideas that come to mind for when you create your ideal state Customer Experience Map. As it gets quite complex, it is very useful to break down and align all such opportunities with each stage of the journey but is an exercise that should be done.

If you want to see an example of the Customer Experience Map for Starbucks please go to www.noelcardona.com/customer-happyland.

MANAGING THE CUSTOMER'S JOURNEY

Businesses change, the marketplace changes and customers change. This only reflects the incredible dynamics challenging nowadays' organisations. What I recommend you do in order to be successful in this critical part of your business, is to put a person or a team in charge of your customer experience so your organisation can:

a. Continuously improve the interactions of your customer and your organisation during their journey.
b. Execute the action plan that must be created once you have your "Current State" and "Ideal State" maps.

c. Collect constant feedback and modify/upgrade the action plan so the results are the ones that the business needs.

d. Ensure that there is someone constantly "travelling" the full Customer Journey, to strengthen and simply the whole system. I call this "someone walking the process". There is nothing more powerful than first-hand experience with a focus on testing standards.

THREE MISTAKES YOU DON'T WANT TO MAKE

As a leader in your organisation, the positive results are attributed to the team but the negatives probably will be placed on you, or at least some times it feels like that.

Everything I have discussed in this book is a framework to achieve a gigantic outcome, which is a sound, long lasting, industry wide recognised business, attracting the best customers and the best team members available. The way I have built this book, as I have said before, is to show you a picture which is normally fragmented in all leaders' minds, because in our heads we tend to disconnect different areas when we actually need to do the opposite: ensure everyone knows they are in the business of delivering happiness. Every member and every department should easily describe what their impact is on Customer Happiness.

To build and maintain this whole framework, an incredible amount of resources are necessary and is there, where you can make three fatal mistakes that you need to avoid.

MISTAKE # 1: LOW PRICES

There is a great book called "Release your breaks" by James Newman, which I would encourage you to read. In this book James discusses how many of us go through life with one foot on the accelerator and the other one  on the brakes. This may be due to fear, ignorance, beliefs, past education, etc. In the same way, many businesses go about trying to deliver the best product or services but, at the same time, competing on price.

In this book I have described a big framework which is necessary to accelerate business excellence and get to Customer Happyland. Building such a framework is not either cheap or easy. The lower you set your prices, the further away you are moving from being able to create unique value and unique experiences.

The cheaper you are, the less your customers will value your products or services and the more you invite people who will give you trouble and affect your business reputation.

The problem of the low prices model is that, it inevitably turns your products or services into a commodity, and these types of products normally have very low margins. With low margins in place, a vicious circle starts where there is not enough money to reinvest in the business for the continuous differentiation, then you keep competing with even lower prices, hurting more and more your business by becoming an even bigger commodity.

As Jason Mars discusses in his "Price Strategy" book, there are actually no commodities, the only thing that exists is Commodity Thinking. In his book Jason refers to several examples, among them, the nancymeyer.com one, which goes to show how something as commoditised as bras and panties can be turned into a specialty. Panties and bras selling for as high as $435 and $460 respectively, go to show this concept. I am pretty sure that for each piece of underwear sold, this business has at least $200 left to invest back into differentiation, by continuously building and strengthening the framework we have discussed in this book. This will move nancymeyer.com a lot faster than any other enterprise with similar products, which only has $2 dollars left to reinvest.

If your mind right now is telling you, "Yes, [your name], I understand this, but the business selling the expensive panties will sell a lot less than the one with cheaper underwear, so the amount to invest may not be as much. You are correct in part, however with every item sold, the non-commoditised business, will attract people with a different mindset (affluent), to whom you can sell more "high ticket" products, creating more revenue and more investment in your business. The commoditised enterprise only yields "cheap" customers always looking for the next bargain.

My whole point with this is the fact that, there is a challenge to overcome, and that is: *average business owners have a mental chain which links production costs with price.* If this chain is not broken, one of the most important fuels necessary to accelerate your business's engine will not be there. By the way, mindset is something we learn from the people we interact with, so be careful who you associate with, and what you allow to get into your head: if 90% of organisations are struggling to get things right, then there is a high likelihood you will find the wrong advice on your way.

Customer happiness has a financial cost which must be taken into account within your business model.

MISTAKE # 2: IMMEDIATE RESPONSE

Imagine this: A surgeon is doing an open heart operation. She starts highly focused, very clear of what the expected outcome is but, 35 mins into the procedure one of the nurses says "Doctor, you have a call from your husband, he  asks if you have a minute for a quick question". What do you think is going to happen here? Obviously somebody is going to get told off for even coming to ask the question. Why this situation brings to our minds the thought "That's not even possible!"? Basically because of the respect that we have for the task the surgeon has at hand.

If we compare the situation above, with our normal day to day, and the fact that 95% of people jump onto the new request instantly, giving immediate response (and forgetting what they were doing), that tells a lot about the way those people operate and the habits they have learned. It tells about the lack of respect they have for the task at hand: they either have no clear goals for that moment in time, or they have it but choose not to achieve them.

The reason I bring this up as a monumental mistake for you as a leader in your business, at the same level at the low prices one, is because it's that important. It is without a doubt, an illness that is eating all modern businesses, and specially augmented by mistake number three which we will discuss shortly.

In the example of the surgeon, we know that she won't accept distractions, either from herself or from anyone in her team, why? Because the team has Ground Level clarity: if they don't focus, if they allow distractions, there will be mistakes that may be fatal. In most business, as we have the notion that if we get it wrong we can always try again, allows the "Have you got a minute" illness to do metastasis.

How is this even related to Customer Happiness? Well, remember I told you that building the framework described here requires resources? We already discussed the financial one, this mistake is about the hours available. The reason this concept is critical, is because you have competition and therefore speed is important, speed is not possible if you are stopping every 5 metres.

This is exactly one of the reasons why, when you work with me, I am not that easy to reach: because I have a tremendous respect for the task at hand and do not allow distractions to side-track me from what I am doing.

MISTAKE # 3: EASY ACCESS

Let's continue with the example of the surgeon. Now in this occasion, the surgeon kept her phone in her pocket. The procedure is going well, the patient is responding, all vital signs are within the expected limits. Right when she is ready to cut into the artery her phone starts vibrating in her pocket giving her a little bit of a scare, unfortunately the artery was severely damaged because of this.

Again this may be unheard of for a surgeon but not for the rest of us. We, many times, sever the artery of our projects because we allow distractions to find us easily.

I am a technology lover but I have come to see how indiscriminate connectivity, which is supposed to increase productivity, is actually doing the opposite.

Easy access is not the same as immediate response, but the likelihood of the latter increases with the presence of the former. The lesson I want to convey here is that, as a leader, you must ensure your organisation goes to the extreme of removing distractions for your team. An example of this is that starting September 2018 the French government has banned mobiles in schools: Pupils can take them to the school but they are not allowed to use them at any point from the beginning to end of the teaching day, not even during breaks.

In order for a business to ensure a continuous accelerating rhythm towards excellence, the leaders across all levels must ensure the environment is purposely managed to allow focused work.

In summary, as a leader, you must work hard to ensure the two most precious resources in a business are managed as the elite in your industry does: *prices to create fuel for customer happiness and time to build the required framework.*

THERE WILL BE UNHAPPY PEOPLE

It is human nature, in any given group there will always be someone who is not completely happy. This is why it is important not to set yourself for failure and aim for 100% happy people.

When I say happy people I mean customers and employees both.

UNHAPPY EMPLOYEES

Some time ago, I read that Microsoft was, at the time, the business with the highest employee happiness score in the world. Dare to guess what the score was (measured from 1 to 10)? It was 7. That is the reason why companies in "The Race" know they must measure first and then aim to improve. If you managed your business by feelings and were asked what level of employee happiness you want to achieve I bet you will say 9 or 10.

There will be people inside your organisation who have engrained deeply in their heads the "moaning and complaining for any reason" because they have slowly drifted in that direction, and is very likely due to the environment they live in. Most of these people can be helped but some others cannot. Somehow you need to find the way to get rid of those who clearly show they cannot be aligned with what you want to do: if you really look hard to what is left out by journalists and idealist writers when they report on Zappos' results, you will manage to find, at some point, something that Tony Hsieh (Zappos' founder) said very clearly: *to increase employee happiness you need to find that 10% who will never be happy and get rid of them.*

UNHAPPY CUSTOMERS

I would actually apply the advice above when it comes to problematic customers. In the same way as with employees, you will have unhappy customers. The only difference is that, arguably, you can fire bad customers easier than bad employees. In the UK, different from the US, you cannot go firing people freely as regulations are more protective.

Customers who decide to keep buying, but at the same time, are never satisfied, are dangerous, because negative feedback can discourage other people from working with you. This is unfair if the lack of satisfaction is due to them and not your business.

THE SOLUTION TO UNHAPPY PEOPLE

The correct solution for this has already been discussed in the book before and it is to do with the upfront filtration you need to do in terms of future customers and employees. The best scenario in terms of unhappy members of your community is not to have them in the first place. Now, if such unhappiness is actually funded, you obviously have to do something about it because it is feedback you must use to improve your business.

The difference between bad customers, which you must keep repelling before and after the relationship has started, with employees, you have it a lot harder if they manage to pass your controls, so I recommend as much time as possible is dedicated to getting the right people for your team. Every minute invested will bring 10, 20 or 50 minutes back in productivity to your business.

SET CLEAR RULES TO FIRE CUSTOMERS

Many employees are abused by unnecessarily rude customers and business leaders will just shake their heads and breathe heavily asking "Why do people need to be so rude?" The issue here is that now you have an upset employee who won't give the best service to the next customer.

For a business to limit the damage done by customers who have managed to bypass your embedded filters, there needs to be crystal clear rules as to what is "customer gross misconduct" and advertise a zero tolerance policy to such behaviours. Then employees can be empowered to report and request a certain person be blocked. The lack of clear limits allows your people to take more and more, until they explode in front of your best customers.

THE NEVER-SATISFIED CUSTOMER

There are certain types of customers who even though don't seem to be unhappy, they are never satisfied and will demand more and more every time, eventually draining your resources. The reason for this may be because they are passing their inefficiency on to you as they don't really plan ahead and end up changing their mind at every step. These types of customers are also dangerous for obvious reasons and therefore it is necessary that you get rid of them. Due to this, you must set clear limits for customer bad behaviour, advertise your zero tolerance policy and, if necessary, don't be afraid to eliminate them from your world.

DISNEY AND CUSTOMER HAPPYLAND

As of 30/09/2017 Disney reported 199,000 employees (with 74,000 of them working at Disney World) and 55 billion US Dollars in revenue. As a business getting close to 100 years in operation. It is certainly a gigantic operation with a very clear vision.

Founded in 1923 by Walt Disney and his brother Roy, this business is now recognised for being a leader in customer happiness and we can learn a lot from how they do it.

I like to highlight from this example the fact that, when we, as customers interact with a business, most of the time we aim for the whole experience to end at the "Satisfaction" level, there are few places we go to, or products or services we buy, with the predetermined intention of being happy. Disney is definitely one of the latter.

Let's have a look at *The Four Journeys* operating seamlessly at Disney to keep this organisation in Customer Happyland. I love having a look at Disney because you can clearly see the four journeys working in unison. If I do a good job here, you will be able to understand more and may be get some ideas to implement in your organisation.

DISNEY'S BUSINESS JOURNEY

I have said before that in order for any journey to go as fast as possible from A to B, there needs to be clarity: *the clearer your vision, the faster you will travel.*

Clarity on what their business is. Walt Disney used to believe in two important things which are necessary to achieve customer happiness. The first one was the definition of what his business was:

"My business is making people, especially children, happy".

The second one was about the scope of the customer experience:

"We provide the whole package".

For Walt, the whole package meant that the Disney experience started from the first call looking for a resort reservation or just for information, until the guest boards the airplane for their trip back home.

In order to transfer that clarity to everyone, Disney has a Service Theme: *"We create happiness by providing the finest in entertainment for people of all ages, everywhere".*

Disney is definitely operating at "The Race" stage. In my book *"The Flood, the Rebirth and The Race"* I discuss the fact that companies at this stage are data driven, Disney is said to secretly be one of the most micromanaged business on the planet. The great thing to notice is that, when people visit their parks, they actually don't see the whole apparatus behind it, it works seamlessly to allow its people to focus on their experience. All this is only possible when a massive amount of process integration, automation and all other three journeys are taken into account.

One of the most important parts of Disney, which fuels all four journeys, is the "Story". This company creates stories and has made sure that all of them are used to create the magic that makes both their employees and customers identify with them. This magic I mention, internally becomes the company culture and externally, it gets people to make the company part of their lives. What this delivers for the business is loyalty on both sides, which is obviously critical for operational excellence and customer happiness.

Disneyland is never finished. Disney understands that being in the elite is not a given, that success is rented and therefore they must keep adding assets to their portfolio. This has a tremendous impact on retention because, for your customers to stay interested, as we discussed in our Four Loops Concept, you must continuously come up with the next widget, the next product or service. On top of that, as Disney is a heavily data driven business, they are continuously using the feedback they get to improve their operations.

Commitment to Quality. In his book "Disney Magic", Rich Hamilton tells of a story of in the early 60's, during the construction of New Orleans Square in Disneyland, Walt ordered the work to be torn up and restarted because he didn't like the way it was going. Was this expensive? Yes, but Walt's response to this was "...I do not worry whether anything is cheap or expensive. We only worry whether is good. I have a theory that if it's good enough, the public will pay us back for it".

If an organisation is committed to excellence at every level, then it is a given that the business will get to "The Race" before its competitors. This is the case of Disney.

DISNEY'S CUSTOMER JOURNEY

One of the ways Disney becomes a story in itself is using their own language. They have a word for the systems that are in place to listen, respond and get to know their customers: *Guestology*. At Disney, Guestology is about getting input constantly and adjust operations quickly.

They listen to them. This connects directly to our Four Loops Concept where Constant Feedback is right at the outer part because it that critical. However, bear in mind that customer feedback tells you whether or not what you are proposing is correct, but you should not fall into the trap of "customer servitude" as we have discussed before. You can tell Disney understands this when they can increase their ticket's price five times in a year with no negative effect on attendance!

The types of feedback methods that Disney uses are for example surveys after customers have gone home, face to face surveys, utilization studies (count what people eat most and what attractions and facilities are used the most). The hard data from these exercises is used to made decisions to optimize operations. For example, the staffing levels of different attractions as well as to align offers with customer's choices such as changing the menu or improving stocking levels to meet demand for a certain food or item, etc. As it stands, Disney has 148,000 ears (74,000 employeesx2☺) paying attention to customers wants and passing the feedback to upper levels. I say this because everyone is encouraged to pass positive and negative feedback up the ladder so improvements can be made.

Another level of feedback gathering at Disney is focus groups. A particular one is called "Creative Advisory council", which is formed by frequent guests, employees or cast members (as they call them) and Imagineers, as they call engineers. (Did I tell you they have their own vocabulary?). These focus groups do deep thinking into new offers, ideas formulated, new merchandise development, etc. The information collected during these focus groups is invaluable.

They Study them. Disney has a particular way to start framing their Customer Map Experience by using their Guest Compass:

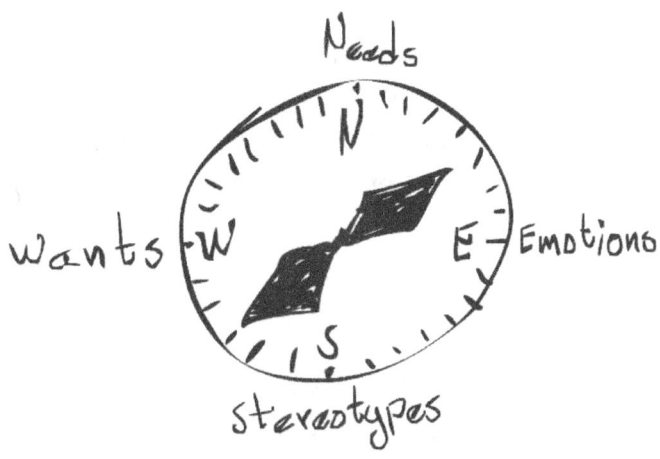

Figure 13. Disney guest compass

This tool is used to analyse the four cardinal points as shown:

- **Needs:** At the basic level, what they actually need and how it can be catered for them like food, water, facilities, shelter, etc.

- **Wants:** Disney knows people go to their parks more due to their wants than their needs. Focus groups are particularly important to really understand how to move from the "Meet my Requirements" base of our Customer Hierarchy of Needs to "Show me Beyond".

- **Stereotypes:** Reviewing the image Disney has created in people's minds and determine if there is anything negative that needs to be fixed. For example, the company goes to great lengths to ensure their parks are extremely clean.

- **Emotions:** Disney is really good at this. Through this exercise, they look at what emotions they want to create during their customer journey and take action to actually do it, as I will explain next.

They Design the Experience. Disney is all about the experience, and they are very clear about what they want their customer to think and especially to feel. For the company, this can be summarised in a phrase: Magic Moments.

A magic moment is either a pre-planned event or one caused by the ongoing training employees receive. Examples of the former are parades where guests are the bulk of the participants who are recruited, given costumes, some dance instructions and then sent to the park's streets. This is very similar to what I described before in the book on customer appreciation events. Examples of what would appear to be "random" magic moments are the result of something I want you to make a note of:

Organisational Culture is created by continuous education and training of employees.

In simple words, employees start creating magic moments as a habit by smiling more, being more helpful, being resourceful when solving unexpected problems for customers, etc.

Zappos is another example where employees are encouraged to make their own decisions when going the extra mile for customers.

A magic moment doesn't have to be a gigantic event, only by smiling more, or asking if you have had a good day, a coffee barista can create a little bit of happiness.

DISNEY'S EMPLOYEE JOURNEY

We have already discussed this a little bit in the section above. As I have said before, Walt Disney used to talk about the whole package, however this whole package was not only for customers, but also for employees.

The system at Disney for managing their employee's Journey is formed by four different strategies:

- People Selection
- People Training
- Communication
- Take Care of the Cast

People Selection. The Disney recruitment process goal is to find people who will thrive within their culture. For this, company's expectations of its employees are shown during the recruitment process. An example is what they call "non-negotiables" such as the "no beard" policy. The idea here is to filter out as many as possible. Behaviour, hobbies, personality, education, etc. are all looked at in order to determine if this person will fit the organisation. Companies in The Race stage will spend an enormous amount of time filtering people out during the recruitment process.

People Training. Disney focuses on three things: the past "Traditions", the current "Operations" and the Company's Vision (Future).

The goal during training is to learn the "Disney Way" and to understand and learn that all actions should lead to create happiness through Magic Moments which is not achieved just by mastering the expected skills.

Bear in mind that this company has recognised training as one of the building pillars of business excellence and has created the *Disney University*, which has standardised training to ensure consistent delivery of what we are discussing here.

The whole training embeds the Employee Journey on what has been, is and will be the Business Journey:

- **"Traditions"**: taught by frontline cast members (employees). It teaches about the history, philosophy, values and traditions of the company. This is a big opportunity to submerge new people into the culture and to start aligning their behaviour with the expected.

- **Current Operations:** Once they know the traditions, people will be sent to the specific business unit they will be working, where their training will take place. Each new recruit is assigned to a person in the recruitment department who will follow up on their training, performance and any adjustments required for the next 6 months.

- **Training for the future:** At Disney, ongoing training is provided and the system is so good that employees can earn a college degree through this process. The more educated your employees are, the better. Another example of this relentless focus on education is a company called The Container Store, which has no limitations for the background of their employees: if an Aerospace Engineer wants to apply for work at one of his stores they will happily consider him, they don't see him as over prepared, on the contrary, it would be a member with high development and intelligence.

Communication. Companies in The Race stage understand the fact that to survive, they need to do marketing to existing and new customers, however they also know for a fact that, "Internal Marketing" is as powerful, and necessary to create a collective mindset where the all the members of the team are aligned with the ideas the leaders want to engrain. Disney understands this very well and it uses many different channels to sell the company's vision, traditions, projects, current customer feedback, recognition to employee's ideas and best practices, etc.

Some of the channels used are highlighted below:

- **Bulletin board.** Placed in strategic areas, allow mid-level managers as well as employees, to communicate important information.

- **Weekly newsletter.** This makes it easy for the company to communicate news, job listings, business projects, customer feedback and, in general, anything which can help run operations more efficiently and brings everyone together such as featuring role model employees.

- **Kiosks with forms and brochures.** Forms that employees would normally have to go and get from the HR department, are located around the parks. Examples are insurance, tax and benefit forms.

- **A Weekly Cast Reference Guide.** Information on the status of projects and schedules, so the cast members have the information required and can answer customer's questions if needed.

- **Annual Cast excellence survey.** An annual exercise to gather accurate feedback from as many employees as possible.

- **Cast Member Communication Log.** A book available to all front staff, which can be used to communicate concerns to their direct management. This is important because as everyone is busy, an idea or feedback can be easily forgotten if not captured immediately.

Taking Care of the Cast. Disney knows what we have discussed before: the way you treat your employees, is the way they will treat your customers. They have actually published that in their internal standards! Taking care of the cast members is all about reinforcing the behaviours that the training and communication discussed before want to engrain. Is the practical side of the strategy if you wish.

- **A positive feedback goal:** Managers need to dispense corrective instruction when needed, however there is a goal to provide at least 3 times more positive feedback than corrective ones.

- **Customer service fanatic cards:** This is an idea that I would encourage you to implement immediately in your business. Disney gives a quote to managers to handout at least 10 recognition cards per day to team members who are doing things really well. The card may look like the one below. After the cast member has been thanked, the card is given to them and they can put it in a special box to win a prize each month during one of the many celebrations Disney has.

Figure 14. Simple recognition card

The manager must keep a record of the given card so additional recognition is given in the form of special pins to those members who have 25, 50, 75 cards. This is a good way to pinpoint your stars within the business.

With the fanatic cards, feedback is given immediately, employees will become emotionally engaged as they will be expecting to receive a prize, and if they win, they will have additional recognition from everyone else. It also develops a habit in managers to go catch people doing things right.

- **Spirit of Disney award:** It is an award which can only be received by a cast member if she is nominated by another team member. It can only be received once in a lifetime and the nominations go through an approval committee. There is a special dinner event where a special pin is presented to the winner and another to the attendees to the night. You can go to this link to see examples and of the pin and how they have evolved during the years.
www.nametagmuseum.com/wdw.html.

- **Disney ambassador:** This is the maximum award for a cast member. In this role, she will represent her resort for a year and her functions will be to do public appearances, guide VIP guests, attend community events, and travel to different places to promote the Disney brand.

- **Partners in excellence:** Another type of award which a team member is nominated for by one of his colleagues. A cast member's committee evaluates whether or not to award the recognition based on three key behaviours: Operational Excellence, Cast Excellence and Guest Satisfaction. Once the prize is awarded, a special banquet is organised and a pin is given. This recognition can be awarded a second time over.

- **Parties and special events:** Disney encourages the sense of family by continuously creating special events which bring the cast together. Boat races, parties, dinners, etc. are all opportunities to get them to interact. The aim is to enhance The Employee Journey by making it fun.

- **Customer letters:** If a customer takes the time to send a letter congratulating the team or an individual, the company will use the opportunity for recognition on billboards, newsletters, etc.

If you carefully analyse some of the strategies used by Disney above, you will notice they have created a sort of "Parallel" ascension path for employees. What

I mean by this is that, even though an employee may not be ascending on the company ladder, they are actually ascending on the "recognition ladder" which also has a gigantic impact on motivation and your "internal customer" (employee) retention.

DISNEY'S SHAREHOLDER'S JOURNEY

Walt Disney certainly didn't envision the Disney Corporation to provide money for him to be able to survive. Even during his worst moments, Walt was obsessed with creating a means of delivering happiness to people. Bear in mind he had to innovate at every step and, what that normally does is to slow things down if the goal is to get rich. However, on the other hand, that way of thinking creates sound foundations to bring long lasting wealth for shareholders. Walt Disney once said on an interview:

"...you reach a point where you don't work for money. Some people worship money as something you've got to have piled up in a big pile somewhere. I've only thought about money in one way, and that 2is to do something with it. I don't think there's a thing I own that I will ever get the benefit of, except through doing things with it".

Now as you probably already know, Walt Disney would have not been able to achieve such business success, and therefore not been able to innovate so much, without the help of his brother Roy Disney, 2 who would keep his feet on the ground while Walt had his heart in the sky.

I have always said that people only achieve the dreams they need, not the ones they just want. You can trace this even to your own life. In the case of Walt, the need was to create, to innovate, to go beyond, without a doubt, this is what kept him alive. In order to be able to have such a life, the way to fulfil those needs had to make commercial sense, and to be financially viable; what he created had to appeal to other people. Finally, he then connected those needs that made him happy (create) with the happiness of other people. That is why his goal, as we have discussed extensively in this book, was to "Create happiness for everyone". Walt passed in Dec 1966 and Roy in Dec 1971, but the company is now stronger than ever. Its current vision statement is

"To be one of the world's leading producers and providers of entertainment and information".

And they keep Walt's mission slogan:

"To make people happy".

I hope this chapter has given you a better understanding of how a company in "The Race" stage, which owns a pretty big piece of territory in Customer Happyland works, and more importantly, ideas to implement out of what you have learned here.

SEMCO PARTNERS AND CUSTOMER HAPPYLAND

This is an example I love, even more that the long discussion we just had on Disney. Before you go further I would like to ask you to go to www.noelcardona.com/customer-happyland and sign in. In the Bronze members area you will find a video called "Capitalising on Happiness". In this video, there is an interview of Ricardo Semler, one of the owners of Semco Partners, which is a Brazilian multinational company dedicated to assembling equipment for the food industry such as pumps, centrifuges, filters, etc. This video is the one that we will be using as a base of the discussion in this chapter.

RICARDO SEMLER'S (SHARHOLDER) JOURNEY

Ricardo Semler did not create this multinational business from scratch. It was inherited. I say this to put things into perspective. Thanks to the financial benefits the business has provided, Ricardo lives in the countryside of Brazil, on a huge estate which has provided the ideal environment to relax. He lives there with his three children and wife.

Ricardo's picture of the world is a different one from many hard capitalists in the globe, for him, the world should revolve around "soft values" such as transparency, trust and love.

It is important to notice that when taking over the business from his father, at a very young age, the company's culture was a more traditional one where people were afraid of losing their jobs if they didn't follow the rules. Still Ricardo, shortly after taking over the business, identified the signs of an organisation which was clearly not in The Race Stage: low morale, not arriving to work on time, fearful, waiting to be told what to do next, Semler himself, describes what his quest was turned in to:

"How to turn someone who needs to be in an organisation, to somebody who actually wants to be there..."

This question was sparked by the fact that when he took over the company in the 80's, he received a business which was operating at a loss, with 220 employees and in a country going through a financial crisis. Obviously there had to be a way to change things around.

Before accepting running this business, Semler put a condition: he wanted absolute autonomy from day one, as he already knew his radical ideas would bring him problems with his father. One of the first measures he put in place was to fire 2/3 of his management structure, naming a teacher as the head of his HR. During the restructuring process, Semler even fired relatives that were working for the company.

Along his Journey, Semler seems to ask very deep questions in terms of whether or not the accepted structure of nowadays' businesses is the most efficient one. He asked questions such as these:

a. What if we leave employees to be responsible for their own salaries?

b. What if they can manage their own time with no start or finish hours?

c. What if you give them all the freedom, even to choose their physical place of work, and only ask about having the discipline to finishing their work on time?

d. What if the profits of the business were shared equally by all employees from bottom to top?

e. What if the most important metric for the business is whether employees really want to go to work on Monday morning, not because they have to, but because they want to?

In a way, Semler has been lucky as when he arrived into the corporate world he had a fresh mind, one not contaminated with the luggage and ideas of everyone who has grown in that environment would have picked up even without realising it. Also, he had a structure in which to apply his theories, which in the first decade yielded a 900% growth. Therefore capitalising on happiness. Also, an important fact to note here is that, the company runs itself without Semler being present in the business, so therefore on the Shareholders Journey, Semler has achieved the Passive Income we discussed in the Shareholder's Hierarchy or Needs, he can now detach from the business and use his time to focus more on his own journey.

During the interview Semler, states:

"I always imagine myself as someone who opens the architecture of the business and then themselves, the people, will arrange the structure in a way they feel comfortable with, which is not at all the way I would be comfortable with. That is why I very much like the idea of setting something up and then going away".

The results achieved at Semco gave him international recognition, invitations to speaking events and being given a guest chair at Harvard.

The fact that Semco Partners doesn't take up Ricardo Semler's time allows him to direct his resources to the top of The Shareholder's Hierarchy of Needs: Changing the world.

Semler explains that, once the business had been tweaked enough, they started to notice that even though people's mentality in the business had changed, the new young employees already came programmed for a need to be controlled and therefore Semler created the Ralston-Semler foundation, which supervises a new type of school. Ricardo calls it Lumiar School, and it's one where 2 year old children are educated in a different way: they can follow their own interests and curiosity. Semler goes to explain how the current school's structure is designed to make it efficient for teachers to manage a group, not for the group to learn. "The current structure is obviously wrong". The goal here is to give them life skills and for them to have autonomy and freedom.

Further on in the documentary, he describes how he is aiming to build a whole community in the area where he lives, for him it's a social experiment. His own words describe a central ideal for the relationship between the shareholder and employee, which allows any business to speed up its journey towards Customer Happyland:

"I want to upgrade their life without downgrading mine."

EMPLOYEE JOURNEY

"Love is what keeps us here", one employee says, and "I am happy with my job", another one comments. The documentary by VPRO follows four employees taking a break at 11:00 am in some comfy hammocks. The break was their decision and the business won't tell them off or take disciplinary action. The reason for them to be able to do this is the company's ethos:

"Do what you like, at your own pace, as long as the work gets done on time".

Thanks to the radical ideas from Semler, The Employee Journey was understood and the business aligned to it. One of the most telling pieces of evidence of the positive impact of the changes was the tremendous growth of the business as well as the total reduction of strikes.

There is a very interesting part of people's psychology exposed through the experience of Semco. Some people have not bought into the philosophy of the business and this is natural part of filtering out people who will never be able to align their beliefs with the ones of the business. Ricardo Semler in the interview, states something I am very aware of and I want you to know as well: For many people, especially those who have been indoctrinated through years of average management theories, it is a lot scarier to have freedom (to be their own managers) than being in an autocratic culture where they are told what to do and to follow strict rules. It may be incredible to believe, but right there you have, a vivid example of how the human mind works and how the concept of happiness is something relative, even something different for each individual.

A final note on The Employee Journey is that employee turnover at Semco is reported to be 2%, 10 times less than the industry average. This shows the impact of these strategies.

THE BUSINESS'S JOURNEY

When Semler took over the business, it had a revenue of $4 million, 20 years after, it has $160 million. That piece of information tells us that the all four journeys at Semco are aligned and yielding the income required. Unfortunately Semler does not go into how the journey to business excellence happened in detail. In a 1994 article for Harvard Business Review, he wrote "participation gives people control of their work, profit sharing gives them a reason to do it better, information tells them what's working and what isn't". He has delegated the entire operation to his people as he has this mindset of "Set it up and let go of it".

What is interesting to see here is how much the impact a well-managed Employee Journey will affect the Customer and Business Journey. It is not enough on its own, but it is very critical.

Leadwise.com published a very interesting interview hosted by Ricardo Semler and Tony Hsieh called "Self-organisation". You can listen to it by signing in to www.noelcardona.com/customer-happyland.

THE CUSTOMER'S JOURNEY

Regrettably there is not much available information on this section from Semco Partners. However, the results and facts I have had access to, definitely show that this part is working.

I have done my best to show you how the four journeys operate under Semco Partners. Once again, it is demonstrated how the four journeys need to be aligned in order to fuel the rocket of your organisation. Do not neglect any of them, otherwise you will be asking why the strategies chased are not yielding the results expected.

FINAL THOUGHTS: OVER TO YOU

My personal definition of happiness is:

"Enjoy what you have and forget about all other options that you have or had".

This can be easily proven when you have a hard time deciding what shoes or shirt to buy, but once you get home, you will forget the other options and you are just happy with your purchase. In fact, if you have ever read about Buddhism for example, the centre of all this practice is that happiness can only be achieved once you remove all expectations from your head, more options are more expectations.

Taking into account this definition of happiness is extremely important, because your aim with your business or organisation is to be able to make your customer either see you as the only option or make them forget about the other ones, it is as simple and as complicated as that.

As one of my mentors says, you need to design your business processes so you can sell in a vacuum. If you don't, your business failure is your fault.

THE GLOBAL LOOP

We have talked about loops before, but there is one you must always keep in mind and is the one shown below:

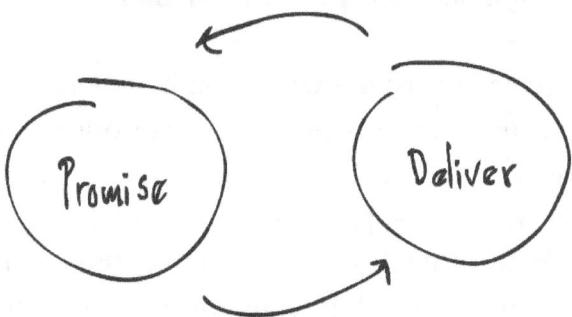

Figure 15. The global loop

It is so critical and simple that you wouldn't think your business would forget it, however it does. Every day businesses promise things they cannot deliver. Sometimes is because they are eager to get a sale out of the door, but most of the time is because the person making the promise simply assumes it can be done and there is no check to confirm this. Do you have these checks in place?

INACCURATE THINKING

This concept goes right back to Napoleon Hill. Simply explained, it means that your concept of right or wrong in any area, in this particular case, in business, is only the result of your current education. Remember the phrase I quoted before "Innovation starts with imitation"? Well, the hidden concept behind it is that we all, every minute of the day, are learning (imitating) what other more successful (or mediocre) people are doing. Even the concept of "successful" can change as we relearn the meaning of such a word and how it applies to our lives. My point with this is that, as a business leader, you must be able to "zoom out" and observe where your current thinking is inaccurate and change it. The best way to do this is by associating with people with different ideas, reading books which challenge the pictures in your head. When do you know your Thinking is Accurate? When you get the results you are looking for!

CUSTOMER HAPPINESS IS NOT AN ISOLATED EVENT

If there is a key point I want to convey with this book is this one: Customer Happiness is the result of the alignment of all your Journeys and all your departments, not the isolated result of your Marketing Department.

If you do the experiment and go and ask your IT department what their impact is on customer happiness, they will struggle to answer, if you ask your production operatives they may give you a standard answer.

The more all your departments understand the mechanics of this "game", the easier it will be to take your company to Customer Happyland.

NO RANDOM EVENTS

There is a hidden concept on this book: in a business which has arrived to Customer Happyland there are no random acts. Every action that is taken has "Ground Level Clarity" and is part of a bigger strategy leading to an extremely well defined gatepost. This undoubtedly starts with its leaders.

As we just discussed, the less isolated your people are from the fact that each one of them affects Customer Happiness, the less you will have random actions in your business.

THE UMBILICAL CORD THEORY

Somebody told me once that we all walk around with our umbilical cord in our hands, looking for a place to connect it to, in other words we are looking for a place to belong. This single need is one that successful businesses take advantage of, to create a base of recurrent revenue which brings stability, and with it, the ability to improve all the four Journeys I have discussed in this book.

Also, as we are all experts in one field, maximum two, in all other areas we look for superheroes, somebody to tell us what to do next. This important aspect is another one which smart business use to increase retention.

THERE IS MORE PROFIT IN RETENTION THAN IN ACQUISITION

Finally, there is a lot of work done in businesses to bring new people to your community and it is certainly easier to keep them with you than it is to go a look for new ones. Effectively, your business will be successful when you understand that the real money is in a business which continuously profits from the relationship with its customers and works heavily to strengthen it: the money you can make through retention is a lot more than that first transaction mediocre businesses focus on.

If I have done my job correctly here, you should have gained incredible clarity as to what really affects Customer Happiness and how to start taking your business there. You should be able to think about **designing, choosing and keeping (your best) customers forever.**

I can always help, but bear in mind I am not an easy person to work with: I will tell you things straight so real improvement is created. I am not easily available to reach because when I work, I have the mindset of the surgeon I talked about before. I am also expensive (My current day fee is £6,000) because I am confident the value you get out of my expertise is 100 times more than what you pay. Also I am normally extremely busy, so you must expect a delay in my response. You can contact me at info@noelcardona.com but please bear in mind I only check that email once a week.

Thank you for the time you have invested in studying this book. My recommendation is that you choose the three most important things you learned and go implement them. If you want to get the free gift I described on the first page on this book, please go to www.noelcardona.com/customer-happyland.

RESOURCES

Books

- The Flood, the Rebirth and the Race. Noel Cardona
- Operations Excellence For Successful CEOs, Noel Cardona
- Conquer the Chaos, Clate Mask
- Delivering Happiness, Tony Hsieh
- Trust Based Marketing, Matt Zagula & Dan Kennedy
- Release your breaks, James Newman
- Price Strategy, Jason Marrs
- Disney Magic, Rich Hamilton
- The Dream Manager, Kelly Matthew

Videos

- Capitalising on Happiness, Ricardo Selmer VPRO documentaries

LIST OF FIGURES

www.ingramcontent.com/pod-product-compliance
Lightning Source LLC
Chambersburg PA
CBHW071431180526
45170CB00001B/300